CONTENTS

I *The Stock that Speaks the Language*
II *The Future of the Language*
III *The English Language in the United States*
IV *The Language in Great Britain*
V *Americanisms Once More*
VI *New Words and Old*
VII *The Naturalization of Foreign Words*
VIII *The Function of Slang*
IX *Questions of Usage*
X *An Inquiry as to Rime*
XI *On the Poetry of Place-Names*
XII *As to "American Spelling"*
XIII *The Simplification of English Spelling*

I
THE STOCK THAT SPEAKS THE LANGUAGE

It is a thousand years since the death of the great Englishman, King Alfred, in whose humble translations we may see the beginnings of English literature. Until it has a literature, however unpretending and however artless, a language is not conscious of itself; and it is therefore in no condition to maintain its supremacy over the dialects that are its jealous rivals. And it is by its literature chiefly that a language forever binds together the peoples who speak it—by a literature in which the characteristics of these peoples are revealed and preserved, and in which their ideals are declared and passed down from generation to generation as the most precious heritage of the race.

The historian of the English people asserts that what made Alfred great, small as was his sphere of action, was "the moral grandeur of his life. He lived solely for the good of his people." He laid the foundations for a uniform system of law, and he started schools, wishing that every free-born youth who had the means should "abide at his book till he can understand English writing." He invited scholars from other lands to settle in England; but what most told on English culture was done not by them but by the king himself. He "resolved to throw open to his people in their own tongue the knowledge which till then had been limited to the clergy," and he "took his books as he found them," the popular manuals of the day, Bede and Boethius and Orosius. These he translated with his own hand, editing freely, and expanding and contracting as he saw fit. "Do not blame me if any know Latin better than I," he explained with modest dignity; "for every man must say what he says and must do what he does according to his ability." And Green, from whom this quotation is borrowed, insists that, "simple as was his aim, Alfred created English literature"—the English literature which is still alive and sturdy after a thousand years, and which is to-day flourishing not only in Great Britain, where Alfred founded it, but here in the United States, in a larger land, the existence of which the good king had no reason ever to surmise.

This English literature is like the language in which it is written, and also like the stock that speaks the language, wherever the race may have planted or transplanted itself, whether by the banks of the little Thames or on the shores of the broad Hudson and the mighty Mississippi. Literature and language and people are practical, no doubt; but they are not what they are often called: they are not prosaic. On the contrary, they are poetic, essentially and indisputably poetic. The peoples that speak English are, and always have been, self-willed and adventurous. This they were long before King Alfred's time, in the early days when they were Teutons merely, and had not yet won their way into Britain; and this they are to-day, when the most of them no longer dwell in old England, but in the newer England here in America. They have ever lacked the restraint and reserve which are the conditions of the best prose; and they have always exulted in the untiring energy and the daring imagination which are the vital elements of poetry. "In his busiest days Alfred found time to learn the old songs of his race by heart," so the historian tells us; "and he bade them be taught in the palace-school."

Lyric is what English literature has always been at its best, lyric and dramatic; and the men who speak English have always been individual and independent, every man ready to fight for his own hand; and the English language has gone on its own way, keeping its strength in spite of the efforts of pedants and pedagogs to bind it and to stifle it, and ever insisting on renewing its freshness as best it could. Development there has been in language and in literature and in the stock itself, development and growth of many kinds; but no radical change can be detected in all these ten centuries. "No national art is good which is not plainly the nation's own," said Mr. Stopford Brooke in his consideration of the earliest English lyrics. "The poetry of England has owed much to the different races which mingled with the original English race; it has owed much to the different types of poetry it absorbed—Greek, Latin, Welsh, French, Italian, Spanish: but below all these admixtures the English nature wrought its steady will. It seized, it transmuted, it modified, it mastered these admixtures both of races and of song."

The English nature wrought its steady will; but what is this English nature, thus set up as an entity and endowed with conscious purpose? Is there such a thing, of a certainty? Can there be such a thing, indeed? These questions are easier to ask than to answer. It is true that we have been accustomed to credit certain races not merely with certain characteristics, but even with certain qualities, esteeming certain peoples to be specially gifted in one way or another. For example, we have held it as an article of faith that the Greeks, by their display of a surpassing sense of form, proved their possession of an artistic capacity finer and richer than that revealed by any other people since the dawn of civilization. And again, we have seen in the Roman skill in constructive administration, in the Latin success in lawmaking and in road-building—we have seen in this the evidence of a native faculty denied to their remote predecessors, the Egyptians. Now come the advocates of a later theory, who tell us that the characteristics of the Greeks and of the Romans are not the result of any inherent superiority of theirs, or of any native predisposition toward art or toward administration, but are caused rather by circumstances of climate, of geographical situation, and of historical position. We are assured now that the Romans, had they been in the place of the Greeks and under like circumstances, might have revealed themselves as great masters of form; while the Greeks, had their history been that of the Romans, would certainly have shown the same power of ruling themselves and others, and of compacting the most diverse nations into a single empire.

No doubt the theory of race-characteristics, of stocks variously gifted with specific faculties, has been too vigorously asserted and unduly insisted upon. It was so convenient and so useful that it could not help being overworked. But altho it is not so impregnable as it was supposed to be, it need not be surrendered at the first attack; and altho we are compelled to abandon the theory as a whole, we can save what it contained of truth. And therefore it is well to bear in mind that even if the Greeks in the beginning had no sharper bent toward art than had the Phenicians,—from whom they borrowed so much of value to be made by them more valuable,—even if their esthetic superiority was the result of a happy chapter of chances, it was a fact nevertheless; and a time came at last when the Greeks were seen to be possessed of a fertility of invention and of a sense of form surpassing all their predecessors had ever exhibited. When this time came the Greeks were conscious of their unexampled achievements and properly proud of them; and they proved that they were able to transmit from sire to son this artistic aptitude—however the aptitude itself had been developed originally. So whether the Roman power to govern and to evolve the proper instruments of government was a native gift of the Latins, or whether it was developed in them by a fortuitous combination of geographical and historical circumstances, this question is somewhat academic, since we know that the Romans did display extraordinary administrative ability century after century. Whenever it was evolved, the artistic type in Greece and the administrative type in Italy was persistent; and it reappeared again and again in successive generations.

This indeed needs always to be remembered, that race-characteristics, whatever their origin, are strangely enduring when once they are established. The English nature whereof Mr. Stopford Brooke speaks, when once it was conscious of itself, worked its steady will, despite the changes of circumstance; and only very slowly is it modified by the accidents of later history and geography. M. Fouillée has set side by side the description of the Germans by Tacitus and the account of the Gauls by Cæsar, drawing attention to the fact that the modern French are now very like the ancient Gauls, and that the descendants of the Germans of old, the various branches of the Teutonic race, have the characteristics of their remote ancestors whom the Roman historian chose to praise by way of warning for his fellow-citizens.

The Romans conquered Gaul and held it for centuries; the Franks took it in turn and gave it their name; but the Gallic type was so securely fixed that the Roman first and then the Frank succumbed to it and were absorbed into it. The Gallic type is not now absolutely unchanged, for, after all, the world does move; but it is readily recognizable to this day. Certain of Cæsar's criticisms read as tho they were written by a contemporary of Napoleon. As Cæsar saw them the Gauls were fickle in counsel and fond of revolutions. Believing in false rumors, they were led into deeds they regretted afterward. Deciding questions of importance without reflection, they were ready to war without reason; and they were weak and lacking in energy in time of disaster. They were cast down by a first defeat, as they were inflamed by a first victory. They were affable, light, inconstant, and vain; they were quick-witted and ready-tongued; they had a liking for tales and an insatiable curiosity for news. They cultivated eloquence, having an astonishing facility of speech, and of letting themselves be taken in by words. And having thus summed up Cæsar's analysis of the Gaul, M. Fouillée asks how after this we can deny the persistence of national types.

What Tacitus has to say of the Germans comes home more closely to us who speak English, since the Teutonic tribes the Latin historian was considering are not more the ancestors of the modern Prussians than they are of the wide-spread Anglo-Saxon peoples. As those who speak English went from the mainland across the North Sea to an island and dwelt there for centuries, and were joined by earlier kin from elsewhere, the race-characteristics were obviously modified a little—just as they have been as obviously modified a little more when some of those who spoke English went out again from the island to a boundless continent across the Atlantic, and were joined here by many others, most of whom were also derived from one or another of the varied Teutonic stocks.

It is nearly two thousand years since Tacitus studied the Teutonic race-characteristics, and yet most of the peculiarities he noted then are evident now. Tacitus tells us that the Teutons were tall, fair-haired, and flegmatic. They were great eaters, not to say gross feeders; and they were given to strong drink. They were fond of games, and were ready to pay their losses with their persons, if need be. They were individual and independent. Their manners were rude, not to call them violent. They were possessed of the domestic virtues, the women being chaste and the husbands faithful. They loved war as they loved liberty. They had a passionate fidelity to their leaders. They decided important questions of policy in public assembly.

The several peoples of our own time who are descended from the Teutons thus described by Tacitus with so sympathetic an insight have been developing for twenty centuries, more or less, each in its own way, under influences wholly unlike, influences both geographical and historical; and it is small wonder that they have diverged as they have, and that no one of them nowadays completely represents the original stock. Some of the points Tacitus made are true to-day in Prussia and are not true in Great Britain; and some hit home here in the United States, altho they miss the mark in Germany. The modern Germans still retain a few of these Tacitean characteristics which the peoples that speak English have lost in their adventurous career overseas. And on the other hand, certain of the remarks of Tacitus might be made to-day in the United States; for example, the willingness to run risks for the fun of the game—is not this a present characteristic of the American as we know him? And here we have always been governed by town-meeting, as the old Teutons were, whereas the modern German is only now getting this back by borrowing it from the English precedent. In our private litigations we continue to abide by the customs of our remote Teutonic ancestors, while the German has accepted as a legal guide the Roman law, wrought out by the countrymen of Tacitus.

Second only to a community of language, no unifying force is more potent than a community of law. In the depths of their dark forests the Teutons had already evolved their own rudimentary code by which they did justice between man and man; and these customary sanctions were taken over to Britain by the Angles and the Saxons and the Jutes; and they served as the foundation of the common law by means of which the peoples that speak English still administer justice in their courts. And here again we find the handiwork of the great King Alfred, from whom we may date the codification of an English law as we may also reckon the establishing of an English literature. With the opportunism of our race, he had no thought of a new legislation, but merely merged the best of the tribal customs into a law for the whole kingdom. The king sought to bring to light and to leave on record the righteous rulings of the wise men who had gone before. "Those things which I met with," so the historian transmits his words, "either of the days of Ine, my kinsman, or of Offa, King of the Mercians, or of Æthelberht, who first among the English race received baptism, those which seemed to me rightest, those I have gathered, and rejected the rest."

Law and language—these are the unrelaxing bands that hold a race firmly together. There are now two main divisions of the Teutonic stock, separated to-day by language and by law—the people who speak German and are ruled by Roman law, and the peoples who speak English and are governed by the common law; and the separation is as wide and as deep legally as it is linguistically. "By the forms of its language a nation expresses its very self," said one of the acutest of British critics; and we have the proof of this at hand in the characteristic differences between the English language and the German. By the forms of its law a people expresses its political beliefs; and we have the evidence of this in the fact that we Americans regard our rulers merely as agents of the town-meeting of the old Teutons, while the modern Germans are submitting to a series of trials for lese-majesty.

Laws have most weight when they are seen to be the expression of the common conscience; and they are most respected when they best reflect the ideals that are "the souls of the nations which cherish them," as a historian of American literature has finely phrased it—"the living spirits which waken nationality into being, and which often preserve its memory long after its life has ebbed away." The marked difference now obvious between the two great divisions of the Teutonic stock—that which speaks English and that which speaks German—is due in part to their not having each conserved exactly the same portion of the ideals inherited from their common ancestors, and in part to their having each acquired other ideals in the course of the many centuries of their separate existence. And the minor differences to be detected between the two great divisions of the stock that speaks English, that dwelling in Great Britain and that dwelling in the United States, are due to similar causes.

While the ancestors of the people who speak German were abiding at home, where Tacitus had seen them, the ancestors of the peoples who speak English went forth across the North Sea and possessed themselves of the better part of Great Britain and gave it a new name. They were not content to defeat the earlier inhabitants in fair fight, and then to leave them in peace, as the Romans did, ruling them and intermarrying with them; the English thrust the natives out violently and harried them away. As Green puts it tersely, "The English conquest for a hundred and fifty years was a sheer dispossession and driving back of the people whom the English conquered." No doubt this dispossession was ruthless; but was it complete? The newcomers took the land for their own, and they meant to kill out all the original owners; but was this possible? The country was rough and thickly wooded, and it abounded in nooks and corners where a family might hide itself. Moreover, what is more likely than that the invader should often spare a woman and take her to wife? For centuries the English kept spreading themselves and pushing back the Britons; but in the long war there were truces now and again, and what is more likely than an incessant intermingling of the blood all along the border as it was slowly driven forward?

Certain it is that one of the influences which have modified the modern English stock is a Celtic strain. If the peoples that speak English are now not quite like the people that speak German, plainly this is one reason: they have had a Celtic admixture, which has lightened them and contributed elements lacking in the original Teuton. To declare just what these elements are is not easy; but to deny their presence is impossible. The Celt has an impetuosity and a swiftness of perception which we do not find in the original Teuton, and which the man who speaks English is now more likely to possess than the man who speaks German. The Celt has a certain shy delicacy; he has a happy sensibility and a turn for charming sentiment; he has a delightful lyric note; and he has at times a sincere and puissant melancholy. These are all qualities which we find in our English literature, and especially in its greatest figure. "The Celts do not form an utterly distinct part of our mixed population," said Henry Morley in a striking passage. "But for early, frequent, and various contact with the race that in its half-barbarous days invented Ossian's dialogues with St. Patrick, and that quickened afterward the Northmen's blood in France, Germanic England would not have produced a Shakspere."

Here we see Morley declaring that the Celt had "quickened the Northmen's blood in France"; and perhaps by his choice of a word he meant to remind us that whereas the Northmen who sailed down the mouth of the Seine were Teutons, the Normans who were to sail up to Hastings had been materially modified during their sojourn in France, which had once been Celtic Gaul. Two series of occasions there were when the English received an accession of Celtic blood: first, when they conquered England; and second, when they in turn were conquered by the Normans, who ruled them for centuries, and were finally merged in them, just as earlier the Romans had been merged in the Gauls. And this recalls to us the fact that there was more in the Norman than the intermingling of the Teuton and the Celt; there was in the Norman also not a little of the Roman who had so long ruled Gaul, and who had so deeply marked it with certain of his own characteristics. Thus it was that the Norman brought into England a Latin tradition; he had acquired something of the Roman administrative skill, something of the Roman's genius for affairs. After the Renascence, Latin influences were to affect the English language and English literature; but it was after the conquest that the English people itself came first in contact with certain of the Roman ideals.

Matthew Arnold thought that we owed "to the Latin element in our language the most of that very rapidity and clear decisiveness by which it is contradistinguished from the modern German"; and he found in the Latinized Normans in England "the sense for fact, which the Celts had not, and the love of strenuousness, clearness, and rapidity, the high Latin spirit, which the Saxons had not." Perhaps the English feeling for style, our command of the larger rhetoric, may be due to this blend of the Norman; and it cannot be denied that this gift has not been granted to the modern German. The fantastic brilliancy of De Quincey and the sonorous picturesqueness of Ruskin are alike inconceivable in the language of Klopstock; and altho there is a pregnant concision in the speeches of Bismarck at his best, there is no German orator who ever attained the unfailing dignity and the lofty affluence of Webster at his best.

Less than two centuries after the good King Alfred had declared English law and established English literature, the Normans came and saw and conquered. Less than three centuries after King William took the land there was born the first great English poet. If the language is to-day what it is, it is because of Chaucer, who chose the court dialect of London to write in, and who made it supple for his own use and the use of the poets that were to come after. The Norman conquest had brought a new and needed contribution to the English character; it had resulted in an immense enrichment of the English language; and it had related English literature again to the broad current of European life. To the original Teutonic basis had been added Celtic and Norman and Latin strains; and still the English nature wrought its steady will, still it expressed itself most freely and most fully in poetry. And in no other poet are certain aspects of this English nature more boldly displayed than in Chaucer, in whom we find a fresh feeling for the visible world, a true tenderness of sentiment, a joyous breadth of humor, and a resolute yet delicate handling of human character.

Two centuries after Chaucer came Shakspere, in whom the English nature finds its fullest expression. The making of England was then complete; all the varied elements had been fused in the fire of a struggle for existence and welded by war with the most powerful of foes. The race-characteristics were then finally determined; and in Elizabethan literature they are splendidly exhibited. Something was contributed by the literature of the Spain that the Elizabethans had stoutly withstood, and something more by the literature of the Italy so many of them knew by travel; but all was absorbed, combined, and assimilated by the English nature, like the contributions that came from the classics of Rome and Greece. Bacon and Cecil, Drake and Ralegh, are not more typical of that sudden and glorious outpouring of English individuality than are Marlowe, Shakspere, and Jonson, Spenser, Chapman, and Massinger. In that greatest period of the race we do not know which is the greater, the daring energy, the enthusiastic impetuosity, the ability to govern, that the English then displayed, or the mighty sweep and range of the imagination as nobly revealed in their poetry. The works of the Elizabethan writers are with us, like the memory of the deeds of the Elizabethan adventurers, as evidence, if any was needful, that the peoples that speak English are of a truth poetic, that they are not prosaic.

In the days of Elizabeth the English began to go abroad and to settle here and there. To those who came to America there were added in due season many vigorous folk from other Teutonic sources; and here in the centuries that have followed was to be seen a fusion of races and a welding into one nation such as had been seen in England itself several centuries earlier. To those who remained in England there came few accretions from the outside, altho when the edict of Nantes was revoked the English gained much that the French lost. The Huguenots were stanch men and sturdy, of great ability often, and of a high seriousness. Some crossed the Channel and some crossed the ocean; and no one of the strands which have been twisted to make the modern American is more worthy than this.

More important than this French contribution, perhaps, was another infusion of the Celtic influence. When the King of Scotland became King of England, his former subjects swarmed to London—preceding by a century the Irishmen who made themselves more welcome in the English capital, with their airy wit and their touch of Celtic sentiment. Far heavier than the Scotch raid into England, and the Irish invasion, was the influx of Scotch, of Irish, and of Scotch-Irish into America. At the very time when Lord Lyndhurst was expressing the opinion that the English held the Irish to be "aliens in blood, aliens in speech, aliens in religion," the Irish were withdrawing in their thousands from the rule of a people that felt thus toward them; and they were making homes for themselves where prejudice against them was not potent. Yet in England itself the Irish left their mark on literature, especially upon comedy, for which they have ever revealed a delightful aptitude; and in the eighteenth century alone the stage is lightened and brightened by the plays of Steele, of Sheridan, and of Goldsmith. About the end of the same century also the Scotch began to make their significant and stimulating contribution to English literature, which was refreshed again by Burns with his breath of sympathy, by Scott with his many-sided charm, and by Byron with his resonant note of revolt.

Just as the Angles and the Saxons and the Jutes had mingled in Great Britain to make the Englishman, and had been modified by Celtic and Norman and Latin influences, so here in the United States the Puritan and the Cavalier, the Dutchman and the Huguenot and the German, the Irish and the Scotch and the Scotch-Irish, have all blended to make the American. Not a few of the original Teutonic race-characteristics recorded by Tacitus are here now, as active as ever; and not a few of the English race-characteristics as revealed by the Elizabethan dramatists survive in America, keeping company with many a locution which has dropped out of use in England itself. There is to-day in the spoken speech of the United States a larger freedom than in the spoken speech of Great Britain, a figurative vigor that the Elizabethans would have relished and understood. It is not without significance that the game of cards best liked by the adventurers who worried the Armada should have been born again to delight the Argonauts of '49. The characteristic energy of the English stock, never more exuberantly displayed than under Elizabeth, suffered no diminution in crossing the Atlantic; rather has it been strengthened on this side, since every native American must be the descendant of some man more venturesome than his kin who thought best to stay at home. Nor is the energy less imaginative, altho it has not taken mainly a literary expression. "There was no chance for poetry among the Puritans," so Lowell reminded us, "and yet if any people have a right to imagination, it should be the descendants of those very Puritans." And he added tersely: "They had enough of it, or they could never have conceived the great epic they did, whose books are States, and which is written on this continent from Maine to California."

More than half those who speak English now dwell in the United States, and less than a third dwell within the British Isles. To some it may seem merely fanciful, no doubt, but still the question may be put, whether the British or the American is to-day really closer to the Elizabethan? It has recently been remarked that the typical John Bull was invisible in England while Shakspere was alive, and that he has become possible in Great Britain only since the day when these United States declared their independence.

Walter Bagehot, the shrewdest of critics of his fellow-countrymen, maintained that the saving virtue of the British people of the middle of the nineteenth century was a stolidity closely akin to stupidity. But surely the Elizabethans were not stolid; and the Americans (who have been accused of many things) have never been accused of stupidity. Mr. Bernard Bosanquet has just been insisting that the two dominant notes of the British character at the beginning of the twentieth century are insularity and inarticulateness. The Elizabethan was braggart and self-pleased and arrogant, but he was not fairly open to the reproach of insularity, nor was he in the least inarticulate. Perhaps insularity and inarticulateness are inseparable; and it may be that it is the immense variety of the United States that has preserved the American from the one, as the practice of the town-meeting has preserved him from the other.

No longer do we believe that there is any special virtue in the purity of race, even if we could discover nowadays any people who had a just right to pride themselves on this. The French are descended from the Gauls, but to the Gauls have been added Romans and Franks; the English are descended from the Teutons, but they have received many accretions from other sources; and the Americans are descended from the British, but it is undeniable that they have differentiated themselves somehow. The admixture of varied stocks is held to be a source of freshness and of renewed vitality; and it may be that this is the cause of the American alertness and venturesomeness. And as yet these foreign elements have but little modified the essential type; for just as the English nature wrought its steady will through the centuries, so the American characteristics have been imposed on all the welter of nationalities that swirl together in the United States.

Throughout the land there is one language, a development of the language of King Alfred, and one law, a development of the law of King Alfred; and throughout the land there are schools such as the good king wished for. American ideals are not quite the same as British ideals, but they differ only a little, and they have both flowered from the English root, as the earlier English ideals had flowered from a Teutonic root. The English stock has displayed in the United States the same marvelous assimilating faculty that it displayed centuries ago in Great Britain, the same extraordinary power of getting the sojourners within its borders to accept its ideals. The law of imitation is irresistible, as M. Tarde has shown; and as M. Fouillée asserts, a nation is really united and unified only when its whole population thrills at the same appeal and vibrates when the same chord is struck. Then there is a consciousness of nationality and of true national solidarity. Throughout the United States there is a unanimous acceptance of the old English ideals—a liking for energy, a respect for character, a belief in equality before the law, and an acceptance of individual responsibility. These are the ideals which will echo again and again in English literature on both shores of the Atlantic, as they have echoed so often since King Alfred died. "A thousand years are but as yesterday when it is past, and as a watch in the night."

(1901)

II
THE FUTURE OF THE LANGUAGE

Two apparently contradictory tendencies are to-day visible. One of them is revealed by our increasing interest in the less important languages and in the more important dialects. The other is to be seen in the immense expansion of the several peoples using the three or four most widely spoken European tongues, an expansion rapidly giving them a supremacy which renders hopeless any attempt of the less important European languages ever to equal them. (It may be noted now once for all that in this paper only the Indo-European languages are taken into account, altho Arabic did succeed for a while in making itself the chief tongue of the Mediterranean basin, overrunning Sicily and even thrusting itself up into Spain, and altho Chinese may have a fateful expansion in the dark future.)

As an instance of the first of the two conflicting tendencies, we have in France the movement of the *félibres* to revive Provençal, and to make it again a fit vehicle for poetry. We have in Norway an effort to differentiate written Norwegian from the Danish, which has hitherto been accepted as the standard speech of all Scandinavian authors. We have in Belgium an increasing resistance to French, which is the official tongue, and an attempt arbitrarily to resuscitate the Flemish dialect. We have in Switzerland a desire to keep alive the primitive and moribund Romansh. We have in North Britain a demand for at least a professorship of broad Scots. We see also that, among the languages of the smaller nations, neither Dutch nor Portuguese shows any symptoms of diminishing vitality, while Rumanian has been suddenly encouraged by the political independence of the people speaking it.

All this is curious and interesting; and yet at the very period when these developments are in progress, other influences are at work on behalf of the languages of the greater races. The developments noted above are largely the work of scholars and of students; they are the artificial products of provincial pride; and they are destined to defeat by forces as invincible as those of nature itself. In their different degrees Provençal and Flemish are struggling for existence against French; but French itself is not gaining in its old rivalry with English and with German.

At the end of the seventeenth century French was the language of diplomacy; it was the speech of the courts of Europe; it was the one modern tongue an educated man in England or in Germany, in Spain or in Italy, needed to acquire. As Latin had been the world-language in the days of the Empire, so French bade fair to be the world-language in the days when all the parts of the earth should be bound together by the bands of commerce and finance. In the eighteenth century the supremacy of French was still indisputable; but in the nineteenth century it disappeared. And, unless all calculations of probability fail us, somewhere in the twentieth century French will have fallen from the first place to the fifth, just below Spanish, just above Italian, and far, far beneath English and Russian and German.

It was the social instinct of the French which made their language so neat, so apt for epigram and compliment, so admirable and so adequate for criticism; and it was the energy of the English-speaking peoples, their individuality, their independence, which made our language so sturdy, so vigorous, so powerful.

An excess of the social instinct it is which has kept the French at home, close to the borders of France, and which has thus restricted the expansion of their language, while it is also an excess of the energy of our stock that has scattered English all over the world, on every shore of all the seven seas. And now that the nineteenth century has drawn to an end, if we can guess at the future from our acquaintance with the past, we are justified in believing that the world-language at the end of the twentieth century—should any one tongue succeed in winning universal acceptance—will be English. If it is not English, then it will not be German or Spanish or French; it will be Russian.

This attempt to foretell the future is not a random venture or a reckless brag; it is based on a comparison of the number of people speaking the different European languages at different periods. At my request Mr. N. I. Stone, of the School of Political Science of Columbia University, made an examination of the statistics, in so far as they are obtainable. The figures are rarely absolutely trustworthy before the nineteenth century—indeed, they are sometimes little better than guesswork. Yet they are approximately accurate, and they will serve fairly well for purposes of comparison. They make plain the way in which one language has gained on another in the past; and they afford material for us to hazard a prediction as to the languages likely to gain most in the immediate future.

In the fourteenth century the population of France was about ten millions, and that of the British Isles probably less than four millions. In both territories there were certainly many who did not speak the chief language; yet the proportion of those who spoke French to those who spoke English was at least ten to four.

Toward the end of the fifteenth century the British Isles still had less than four millions, while France had more than twelve millions. At this same period Italy had a few more than nine millions, and Spain a few less, while the Germans (including always the Austrians who spoke German) were about ten millions.

Coming toward the end of the sixteenth century, we find six millions in the British Isles, more than fourteen millions in France and in the French-speaking portions of the adjacent countries, and more than ten millions in Italy. The Russians then numbered nearly four millions and a half—only a million and a half less than the British.

At the very end of the seventeenth century the number of those speaking English was nearly eight millions and a half—most of them still in the British Isles, but some of them already departed into the colonies in America and elsewhere. The number of those speaking French was twenty millions, of those speaking Italian a few less than twelve millions, and of those speaking Russian about fifteen millions. Those speaking Spanish were chiefly at home in the Iberian peninsula, but not a few were in the colonies in America: they amounted to about eight millions in all, the mother-country having wasted her people in ruinous wars.

At the very end of the eighteenth century we find the English-speaking peoples on both shores of the Atlantic swollen to twenty-two millions, having nearly trebled in a hundred years, while the French had added only a third to their population, amounting in all to a few more than twenty-seven millions. The Germans were about thirty-three millions, having passed the French; and the Italians were a few more than thirteen millions, having increased very slowly. Neither Germans nor Italians had as yet been able either to achieve unity for themselves or to found colonies elsewhere. The Spanish, including their pure-blooded colonists, numbered perhaps ten millions. The Russians had increased to twenty-five millions, the boundaries of their empire having been widely extended.

The nineteenth century was a period of unexampled expansion for the English-speaking race, who have spread to India, to Australia, and to Africa, besides filling up the western parts of the United States; they now number probably between a hundred and twenty-five and a hundred and thirty millions. The Russians have also pushed their borders across Asia, and they also show an immense increase, now numbering about a hundred and thirty millions, altho probably a very large proportion of their conglomerate population does not yet speak Russian. The Germans have supplied millions of immigrants to the United States, and thousands of expatriated traders to all the great cities of the world; and in spite of this loss they now number about seventy millions (including, as before, the German portions of the Austro-Hungarian monarchy). The Spanish-speaking peoples in the old world and the new are about forty-two millions, not half of them being in Spain itself.

The French lag far behind in this multiplication; they number now a few more than forty millions, including those Belgians and Swiss who have French for their mother-tongue. The relative loss of the French can best be shown by a comparison with the English after an interval of five hundred years. In the fourteenth century, as we have seen, those who spoke French were to those who spoke English as ten to four; in the nineteenth century those who speak English are to those who speak French as one hundred and thirty to forty. In other words, the French during five centuries have increased fourfold, while the English have multiplied more than thirtyfold.

French is still the language most frequently employed by diplomatists; it is still the tongue in which educated men of differing nationalities are most likely to be able to converse with each other. But its supremacy has departed forever. It has long been fighting a losing battle. Its hope of becoming the world-language of the future vanished, never to reappear, when Clive grasped India and when Wolfe defeated Montcalm. At a brief interval the French let slip their final chances of holding either the east or the west.

The English-speaking peoples and the Russians have entered into the inheritance which the French have renounced. The future is theirs, for they are ready to go forth and subdue the waste places of the earth. They are the great civilizing forces of the twentieth century, each in its own way and each in its own degree. The Russians have revealed a remarkable faculty of assimilation, and have taken over the wild tribes of the east, which they are slowly starting along the path of progress. The English—by which I mean always the peoples who speak the English language—have possessed themselves of North America and of South Africa and of Australia; and there is no sign yet visible of any lack of energy or of any decrease of vigor in the branches of this hardy and prolific stock.

At the rate of increase of the nineteenth century, the end of the twentieth century will find eight hundred and forty millions speaking English and five hundred millions speaking Russian, while those who speak German will be one hundred and thirty millions and those who speak French perhaps sixty millions. But it is very unlikely that the rate of increase in the twentieth century will be what it was in the nineteenth. The extraordinary expansion of the United States is the salient phenomenon of the nineteenth century; and it is doubtfully possible and certainly improbable that any such expansion can take place in the twentieth century, even in South Africa. On the other hand, the building of the Siberian railroad may open to the Russians an outlet for the overflow of their population not unlike that offered to the English by the opening of the middle west of the United States. The outpouring of Germans, hitherto directed chiefly to the United States (where they have been taught to speak English), may perhaps hereafter be diverted to German colonies, where the native tongue will be cherished.

Thus it seems likely that, while the estimate for the year 2000 of one hundred and thirty million Germans is none too large, that of five hundred million Russians is perhaps too small, and that of eight hundred and fifty millions for the English-speaking peoples is probably highly inflated. What, however, we have no reasonable right to doubt is that German will be a bad third, as French will be a bad fourth; and that the English language and the Russian will stand far at the head of the list, one all-powerful in the west and the other all-powerful in the east. Which of them will prevail against the other in the twenty-first century no man can now foretell, nor can he get any help from statistics.

The issue of that conflict cannot be foreseen by any inspection of figures, for it will turn not so much on mere numbers—altho the possession of these will be an immense advantage: it will be decided rather by the race-characteristics of the two stocks when thrust into irresistible opposition. The manners and customs of the people who speak Russian and of the peoples who speak English, their physical strength and their vitality, their ideals, social and political—all these things will be the decisive factors in the final combat. Whether Russian or English shall be the world-language of the future depends not on the language itself and its merits and demerits, but on the sturdiness of those who shall then speak it, on their strength of will, on their power of organization, on their readiness to sacrifice themselves for the common cause, and on their fidelity to their ideals.

Russian is a beautiful language, so those say who know it best: it is fresh and vigorous, as might be expected in a speech the literature of which is not yet old; it is also as clear and as direct as French. But it has one insuperable disadvantage: its grammar is as primitive and as complex as the grammar of German or the grammar of Greek. The verb has an elaborate conjugation, the noun an elaborate declension, the adjective an elaborate method of agreement in gender, number, and case.

Now English is fortunate in having discarded nearly all this primitive machinery, which is always a sign of linguistic immaturity. The English language has shed almost all its unnecessary complications; it has advanced from complexity toward simplicity, while Russian still lingers in its unreformed condition of arbitrary elaboration. One objection, it may be noted, to Volapük, which a German scholar kindly invented as the world-language of the future, was that its grammar was of this primitive and complicated type.

In these days of the printing-press and of the schoolmaster any radical modification of the mother-tongue is increasingly difficult, so that it is highly improbable that Russian can now ever shake off these grammatical encumbrances that really unfit it for use as a world-language to be acquired by all men. Russian is one of the most backward of modern languages in its progress toward grammatical simplicity; and English is one of the most forward. Italian is also a language which had the good fortune partly to reform its grammar before the invention of printing made the operation almost impossible; and Italian is like English in that it is a very easy language to learn by word of mouth, as the rules of grammar we must needs obey are very few,—tho in this respect English is superior even to Italian. If English is hard to learn when it is taught by the eye instead of the ear, this is because of our cumbersome and antiquated spelling; here the Italian is far better off than the English.

Indeed, it is not a little strange that the English language, which is one of the most advanced in grammatical simplicity, is one of the most belated in orthographic simplicity. In no other modern language is the system of spelling—if system that can be called which has no rule or reason—more arbitrary and more chaotic than in English; and no other peculiarity of our language does more to retard its diffusion than its wantonly foolish orthography.

Probably much of the violent opposition to the simplification of our spelling is due to the fanatic zeal of the phonetic reformers, who have frightened away all the timid respecters of tradition by their rash insistence upon the immediate adoption of some brand-new and comprehensive scheme. The English-speaking peoples are essentially conservative and unfailingly opportunist; they abhor all radical remedies. They are wont to remove ancient abuses piecemeal, and not root and branch. The most they can be got to do in the immediate future is to follow the example of the Italians, and to lop off gradually the most flagrant inconsistencies and absurdities of our present spelling, here a little and there a little, going forward hesitatingly, but never stopping.

In this good work of injecting a little more sense into our orthography, as in the other good work of still further simplifying our grammar as occasion serves and opportunity offers, we Americans may have to take the lead. The English language is ours by inheritance, and our interest in it is as deep and as wide as that of our British cousins. As Mark Twain has put it, with his customary shrewdness, it is "the King's English" no longer, for it has gone into the hands of a company, and a majority of the stock is held on our side of the Atlantic.

We Americans must awake to a sense of our responsibility as the chief of the English-speaking peoples. The tie that binds the British colonies to the British crown is strong only because it is loose; and in Australia and in Canada the conditions of life resemble those of the United States rather than those of Great Britain. The British Isles are the birthplace of our race, but they no longer contain the most important branch of the English-speaking peoples. On both sides of the Atlantic, and afar in the Pacific also, and along the shores of the Indian Ocean, are "the subjects of King Shakspere," the students of Chaucer and Dryden, the readers of Scott and Thackeray and Hawthorne; but most of them, or at least the largest single group, will be in the United States at the end of the twentieth century, as they are at the end of the nineteenth.

No one has more clearly seen the essential unity of the English-speaking race, and no one has more accurately stated the relation of the American branch of this race to the British branch, than the late John Richard Green. In his chapter on the independence of America, he recorded the fact that since 1776 "the life of the English people has flowed not in one current, but in two; and while the older has shown little sign of lessening, the younger has fast risen to a greatness which has changed the face of the world. In wealth and material energy, as in numbers, it far surpasses the mother-country from which it sprang. It is already the main branch of the English people; and in the days that are at hand the main current of that people's history must run along the channel, not of the Thames or the Mersey, but of the Hudson and the Mississippi."

When English becomes the world-language,—if our speech ever is raised to fill that position of honor and usefulness,—it will be the English language as it is spoken by all the branches of the English race, no doubt; but the dominant influence in deciding what the future of that language shall be must come from the United States. The English of the future will be the English that we shall use here in the United States; and it is for us to hand it down to our children fitted for the service it is to render.

This task is ours, not to be undertaken boastfully or vaingloriously or in any spirit of provincial self-assertion, on the one hand, or of colonial self-depreciation on the other, but with a full sense of the burden imposed upon us and of the privilege that accompanies it. It is our duty to do what we can to keep our English speech fresh and vigorous, to help it draw new life and power from every proper source, to resist all the attempts of pedants to cramp it and restrain its healthy growth, and to urge along the simplification of its grammar and its orthography, so that it shall be ready against the day when it is really a world-language.

(1898)

III
THE ENGLISH LANGUAGE IN THE UNITED STATES

When Benjamin Franklin was in England in 1760, he received a letter from David Hume commenting on the style of an essay of his writing and on his choice of words; and in his reply Franklin modestly thanked his friend for the criticism, and took occasion to declare his hope that we Americans would always "make the best English of this island our standard." And yet when France acknowledged the independence of the United States in 1778 and Franklin was sent to Paris as our minister, Congress duly considered the proper forms and ceremonies to be observed in doing business with foreign countries, and finally resolved that "all speeches or communications may, if the public ministers choose it, be in the language of their respective countries; and all replies or answers shall be in the language of the United States."

What is "the language of the United States"? Is it "the best English" of Great Britain, as Franklin hoped it would always be? Franklin was unusually far-sighted, but even he could not foresee what is perhaps the most extraordinary event of the nineteenth century,—an era abounding in the extraordinary,—the marvelous spread and immense expansion of the English language. It is not only along the banks of the Thames and the Tweed and the Shannon that children are now losing irrecoverable hours on the many absurdities of English orthography: a like wanton wastefulness there is also on the shores of the Hudson, of the Mississippi, and of the Columbia, while the same A B C's are parroted by the little ones of those who live where the Ganges rolls down its yellow sand and of those who dwell in the great island which is almost riverless. No parallel can be found in history for this sudden spreading out of the English language in the past hundred years—not even the diffusion of Latin during the century when the rule of Rome was most widely extended.

Among the scattered millions who now employ our common speech, in England itself, in Scotland, Wales, and Ireland, in the United States and

Canada, in India and in Australia, in Egypt and in South Africa, there is no stronger bond of union than the language itself. There is no likelihood that any political association will ever be sought or achieved. The tie that fastens the more independent colonies to the mother-country is loose enough now, even if it is never further relaxed; and less than half of those who have English for their mother-tongue owe any allegiance whatever to England. The English-speaking inhabitants of the British Empire are apparently fewer than the inhabitants of the American republic; and the population of the United Kingdom itself is only a little more than half the population of the United States.

To set down these facts is to point out that the English language is no longer a personal possession of the people of England. The power of the head of the British Empire over what used to be called the "King's English" is now as little recognized as his power over what used to be called the "king's evil." We may regret that this is the case, or we may rejoice at it; but we cannot well deny the fact itself. And thus we are face to face with more than one very interesting question. What is going to become of the language now it is thus dispersed abroad and freed from all control by a central authority and exposed to all sorts of alien influences? Is it bound to become corrupted and to sink from its high estate into a mire of slang and into a welter of barbarously fashioned verbal novelties? What, more especially, is going to be the future of the English language here in America? Must we fear the dread possibility that the speech of the peoples on the opposite sides of the Western Ocean will diverge at last until the English language will divide into two branches, those who speak British being hardly able to understand those who speak American, and those who speak American being hardly able to understand those who speak British? Mark Twain is a humorist, it is true, but he is very shrewd and he has abundant common sense; and it was Mark Twain who declared a score of years ago that he spoke the "American language."

The science of linguistics is among the youngest, and yet it has already established itself so firmly on the solid ground of ascertained truth that it has been able to overthrow with ease one and another of the many theories which were accepted without question before it came into being. For example, time was—and the time is not so very remote, it may be remarked —time was when the little group of more or less highly educated men who were at the center of authority in the capital of any nation had no doubt whatsoever as to the superiority of their way of speaking their own language over the manner in which it might be spoken by the vast majority of their fellow-citizens deprived of the advantages of a court training. This little group set the standard of speech; and the standard they set was accepted as final and not to be tampered with under penalty of punishment for the crime of lese-majesty. They held that any divergence from the customs of speaking and writing they themselves cherished was due to ignorance and probably to obstinacy. They believed that the court dialect which they had been brought up to use was the only true and original form of the language; and they swiftly stigmatized as a gross impropriety every usage and every phrase with which they themselves did not happen to be familiar. And in thus maintaining the sole validity of their personal habits of speech they had no need for self-assertion, since it never entered into the head of any one not belonging to the court circle to question for a second the position thus tacitly declared.

Yet if modern methods of research have made anything whatever indisputable in the history of human speech, they have completely disproved the assumption which underlies this implicit claim of the courtiers. We know now that the urban dialect is not the original language of which the rural dialects are but so many corruptions. We know, indeed, that the rural dialects are often really closer to the original tongue than the urban dialect; and that the urban dialect itself was once as rude as its fellows, and that it owes its preëminence rarely to any superiority of its own over its rivals, but rather to the fact that it chanced to be the speech of a knot of men more masterful than the inhabitants of any other village, and able therefore to expand their village to a town and at last to a city, which imposed its rule on the neighboring villages, the inhabitants of these being by that time forgetful that they had once striven with it on almost equal terms. Generally it is the stability given by political pre-eminence which leads to the development of a literature, without which no dialect can retain its linguistic supremacy.

When the sturdy warriors whose homes were clustered on one or another of the seven hills of Rome began to make alliances and conquests, they rendered possible the future development of their rough Italic into the Latin language which has left its mark on almost every modern European tongue.

The humble allies of the early Romans, who possessed dialects of an equal antiquity and of an equal possibility of improvement, could not but obey the laws of imitation; and they sought, perforce, to bring their vocabulary and their syntax into conformity with that of the men who had shown themselves more powerful. Thus one of the Italic dialects was singled out by fortune for an extraordinary future, and the other Italic dialects were left in obscurity, altho they were each of them as old as the Roman and as available for development. These other dialects have even suffered the ignominy of being supposed to be corruptions of their triumphant brother.

The French philologist Darmesteter concisely explained the stages of this development of one local speech at the expense of its neighbors. As it gains in dignity its fellows fall into the shadow. A local speech thus neglected is a patois; and a local speech which achieves the dignity of literature is a dialect. These written tongues spread on all sides and impose themselves on the surrounding population as more noble than the patois. Thus a linguistic province is created, and its dialect tends constantly to crush out the various patois once freely used within its boundaries.

In time one of these provinces becomes politically more powerful than the others and extends its rule over one after another of them. As it does this, its dialect replaces the dialects of the provinces as the official tongue, and it tends constantly to crush out these other dialects, as they had tended constantly to crush out the various patois. Thus the local speech of the population of the tiny island in the Seine, which is the nucleus of the city of Paris, rose slowly to the dignity of a written dialect, and the local speech of each of the neighboring villages sank into a patois—altho originally it was in no wise inferior. In the course of centuries Paris became the capital of France, and its provincial dialect became the official language of the kingdom. When the kings of France extended their rule over Normandy and over Burgundy and over Provence, the Parisian dialect succeeded in imposing itself upon the inhabitants of those provinces as superior; and in time the Norman dialect and the Burgundian and the Provençal were ousted.

The dialect of the province in which the king dwelt and in which the business of governing was carried on, could not but dispossess the dialects of all the other provinces; and thus the French language, as we know it now, was once only the Parisian dialect. Yet there was apparently no linguistic inferiority of the *langue d'oc* to the *langue d'oil*; and the reasons for the dominion of the one and the decadence of the other are purely political. Of course, as the Parisian dialect grew and spread itself, it was enriched by locutions from the other provincial dialects, and it was simplified by the dropping of many of its grammatical complexities not common to the most of the others.

The French language was developed from one particular provincial dialect probably no better adapted for improvement than any one of half a dozen others; but it is to-day an instrument of precision infinitely finer than any of its pristine rivals, since they had none of them the good fortune to be chosen for development. But the patois of the peasant of Normandy or of Brittany, however inadequate it may be as a means of expression for a modern man, is not a corruption of French, any more than Doric is a corruption of Attic Greek. It is rather in the position of a twin brother disinherited by the guile of his fellow, more adroit in getting the good will of their parents. It was the literary skill of the Athenians themselves, and not the superiority of the original dialect, that makes us think of Attic as the only genuine Greek, just as it was the prowess of the Romans in war and their power of governing which raised their provincial dialect into the language of Italy, and then carried it triumphant to every shore of the Mediterranean.

The history of the development of the English language is like the history of the development of Greek and Latin and French; and the English language as we speak it to-day is a growth from the Midland dialect, itself the victor of a struggle for survivorship with the Southern and Northern dialects. "With the accession of the royal house of Wessex to the rule of Teutonic England," so Professor Lounsbury tells us, "the dialect of Wessex had become the cultivated language of the whole people—the language in which books were written and laws were published." But when the Norman conquest came, altho, to quote from Professor Lounsbury again, "the native tongue continued to be spoken by the great majority of the population, it went out of use as the language of high culture," and "the educated classes, whether lay or ecclesiastical, preferred to write either in Latin or in French —the latter steadily tending more and more to become the language of literature as well as of polite society." And as a result of this the West-Saxon had to drop to the low level of the other dialects; "it had no longer any preëminence of its own." There was in England from the twelfth to the fourteenth centuries no national language, but every one was free to use with tongue and pen his own local speech, altho three provincial dialects existed, "each possessing a literature of its own and each seemingly having about the same chance to be adopted as the representative national speech."

These three dialects were the Southern (which was the descendant of Wessex, once on the way to supremacy), the Northern, and the Midland (which had the sole advantage that it was a compromise between its neighbors to the north and the south). London was situated in the region of the Midland dialect, and it was therefore "the tongue mainly employed at the court" when French slowly ceased to be the language of the upper classes. As might be expected in those days before the printing-press and the spelling-book imposed uniformity, the Midland dialect was spoken somewhat differently in the Eastern counties from the way it was spoken in the Western counties of the region. London was in the Eastern division of the Midland dialect, and London was the capital. Probably because the speech of the Eastern division of the Midland dialect was the speech of the capital, it was used as the vehicle of his verse by an officer of the court—who happened also to be a great poet and a great literary artist. Just as Dante's choice of his native Tuscan dialect controlled the future development of Italian, so Chaucer's choice controlled the future development of English. It was Chaucer, so Professor Lounsbury declares, "who first showed to all men the resources of the language, its capacity of representing with discrimination all shades of human thought and of conveying with power all manifestations of human feeling."

The same writer tells us that "the cultivated English language, in which nearly all English literature of value has been written, sprang directly from the East-Midland division of the Midland dialect, and especially from the variety of the East-Midland which was spoken at London and the region immediately to the north of it." That this magnificent opportunity came to the London dialect was not due to any superiority it had over any other variety of the Midland dialect: it was due to the single fact that it was the speech of the capital—just as the dialect of the Île-de-France in like manner served as the stem from which the cultivated French language sprang. The Parisian dialect flourished and imposed itself on all sides; within the present limits of France it choked out the other local dialects, even the soft and lovely Provençal; and beyond the boundaries of the country it was accepted in Belgium and in Switzerland.

So the dialect of London has gone on growing and refining and enriching itself as the people who spoke it extended their borders and passed over the wide waters and won their way to far countries, until to-day it serves not merely for the cockney Tommy Atkins, the cow-boy of Montana, and the larrikin of Melbourne: it is adequate for the various needs of the Scotch philosopher and of the American humorist; it is employed by the Viceroy of India, the Sirdar of Egypt, the governor of Alaska, and the general in command over the Philippines. In the course of some six centuries the dialect of a little town on the Thames has become the mother-tongue of millions and millions of people scattered broadcast over the face of the earth.

If the Norman conquest had not taken place the history of the English race would be very different, and the English language would not be what it is, since it would have had for its root the Wessex variety of the Southern dialect. But the Norman conquest did take place, and the English language has for its root the Eastern division of the Midland dialect. The Norman conquest it was which brought the modest but vigorous young English tongue into close contact with the more highly cultivated French. The French spoken in England was rather the Norman dialect than the Parisian (which is the true root of modern French), and whatever slight influence English may have had upon it does not matter now, for it was destined to a certain death. But this Norman-French enlarged the plastic English speech against which it was pressing; and English adopted many French words, not borrowing them, but making them our own, once for all, and not dropping the original English word, but keeping both with slight divergence of meaning.

Thus it is in part to the Norman conquest that we owe the double vocabulary wherein our language surpasses all others. While the framework of English is Teutonic, we have for many things two names, one of Germanic origin and one of Romance. Our direct, homely words, that go straight to our hearts and nestle there—these are most of them Teutonic. Our more delicate words, subtle in finer shades of meaning—these often come to us from the Latin through the French. The secondary words are of Romance origin, and the primary words of Germanic. And this—if the digression may here be hazarded—is one reason why French poetry touches us less than German, the words of the former seeming to us remote, not to say sophisticated, while the words of the latter are akin to our own simpler and swifter words.

One other advantage of the pressure of French upon English in the earlier stages of its development, when it was still ductile, was that this pressure helped us to our present grammatical simplicity. Whenever the political intelligence of the inhabitants of the capital of a district raises the local dialect to a position of supremacy, so that it spreads over the surrounding districts and casts their dialects into the shadow, the dominant dialect is likely to lose those of its grammatical peculiarities not to be found also in the other dialects. Whatever is common to them all is pretty sure to survive, and what is not common may or may not be given up. The London dialect, in its development, felt the influence, not only of the other division of the Midland dialect, and of the two rival dialects, one to the north of it and the other to the south, but also of a foreign tongue spoken by all who pretended to any degree of culture. This attrition helped English to shed many minor grammatical complexities still retained by languages which had not this fortunate experience in their youth.

Perhaps the late Richard Grant White was going a little too far when he asserted that English was a grammarless tongue; but it cannot be denied that English is less infested with grammar than any other of the great modern languages. German, for example, is a most grammarful tongue; and Mark Twain has explained to us (in 'A Tramp Abroad') just how elaborate and intricate its verbal machinery is; and the Volapük, which was made in Germany, had the syntactical convolutions of its inventor's native tongue.

By its possession of this grammatical complexity, Volapük was unfitted for service as a world-language. A fortunate coincidence it is that English, which is becoming a world-language by sheer force of the energy and determination of those whose mother-speech it is, should early have shed most of these cumbersome and retarding grammatical devices. The earlier philologists were wont to consider this throwing off of needless inflections as a symptom of decay. The later philologists are coming to recognize it as a sign of progress. They are getting to regard the unconscious struggle for short-cuts in speech, not as degeneration, but rather as regeneration. As Krauter asserts, "The dying out of forms and sounds is looked upon by the etymologists with painful feelings; but no unprejudiced judge will be able to see in it anything but a progressive victory over lifeless material." And he adds, with terse common sense: "Among several tools performing equal work, that is the best which is the simplest and most handy." This brief excerpt from the German scholar is borrowed here from a paper prepared for the Modern Language Association by Professor C. A. Smith, in which may be found also a dictum of the Danish philologist Jespersen: "The fewer and shorter the forms, the better; the analytic structure of modern European languages is so far from being a drawback to them that it gives them an unimpeachable superiority over the earlier stages of the same languages." And it is Jespersen who boldly declares that "the so-called full and rich forms of the ancient languages are not a beauty, but a deformity."

In other words, language is merely an instrument for the use of man; and like all other instruments, it had to begin by being far more complicated than is needful. The watch used to have more than a hundred separate parts, and now it is made with less than twoscore, losing nothing in its efficiency and in precision. Greek and German are old-fashioned watches; Italian and Danish and English are watches of a later style. Of the more prominent modern languages, German and Russian are the most backward, while English is the most advanced. And the end is not yet, for the eternal forces are ever working to make our tongue still easier. The printing-press is a most powerful agent on the side of the past, making progress far more sluggish than it was before books were broadcast; yet the English language is still engaged in sloughing off its outworn grammatical skin. Altho in the nineteenth century the changes in the structure of English have probably been less than in any other century of its history, yet there have been changes not a few.

For example, the subjunctive mood is going slowly into innocuous desuetude; the stickler for grammar, so-called, may protest in vain against its disappearance: its days are numbered. It serves no useful purpose; it has to be laboriously acquired; it is now a matter of rule and not of instinct; it is no longer natural: and therefore it will inevitably disappear, sooner or later. Careful investigation has shown that it has already been discarded by many even among those who are very careful of their style—some of whom, no doubt, would rise promptly to the defense of the form they have been discarding unconsciously. One authority declares that altho the form has seemed to survive, it has been empty of any distinct meaning since the sixteenth century.

This is only one of the tendencies observable in the nineteenth century; and we may rest assured that others will become visible in the twentieth. But when English is compared with German, we cannot help seeing that most of this work is done already. Grammar has been stripped to the bone in English; and for us who have to use the language to-day it is fortunate that our remote ancestors, who fashioned it for their own use without thought of our needs, should have had the same liking we have for the simplest possible tool, and that they should have cast off, as soon as they could, one and another of the grammatical complexities which always cumber every language in its earlier stages, and most of which still cumber German. In nothing is the practical directness of our stock more clearly revealed than in this immediate beginning upon the arduous task of making the means of communication between man and man as easy and as direct as possible. Doubly fortunate are we that this job was taken up and put through before the invention of printing multiplied the inertia of conservatism.

It was the political supremacy of Paris which made the Parisian dialect the standard of French; and it was the genius of Dante which made the Tuscan dialect the standard of Italian. That the London dialect is the standard of English is due partly to the political supremacy of the capital and partly to the genius of Chaucer. As the French are a home-keeping people, Paris has retained its political supremacy; while the English are a venturesome race and have spread abroad and split into two great divisions, so that London has lost its political supremacy, being the capital now only of the less numerous portion of those who have English as their mother-tongue.

It is true, of course, that a very large proportion of the inhabitants of the United States, however independent politically of the great empire of which London is the capital, look with affection upon the city by the Thames. Their feeling toward England is akin to that which led Hawthorne to entitle his record of a sojourn in England 'Our Old Home.' The American liking for London itself seems to be increasing; and, as Lowell once remarked, "We Americans are beginning to feel that London is the center of the races that speak English, very much in the sense that Rome was the center of the ancient world." It was at a dinner of the Society of Authors that he said this, and he then added: "I confess that I never think of London, which I also confess I love, without thinking of the palace David built, 'sitting in the hearing of a hundred streams'—streams of thought, of intelligence, of activity."

While the London dialect is the stem from which the English language has grown, the vocabulary of the language has never been limited by the dialect. It has been enriched by countless words and phrases and locutions of one kind or another from the other division of the Midland dialect and from both the Northern and the Southern dialects—just as modern Italian has not limited itself to the narrow vocabulary of Florence. Yet in the earlier stages of the development of English the language benefited by the fact that there was a local standard. The attempt of all to assimilate their speech to that of the inhabitants of London tended to give uniformity without rigidity. As men came up to court they brought with them the best of the words and turns of speech peculiar to their own dialect; and the language gained by all these accretions.

Shakspere contributed Warwickshire localisms not a few, just as Scott procured the acceptance of Scotticisms hitherto under a ban. As Spenser had gone back to Chaucer, so Keats went to the Elizabethans and dug out old words for his own use; and William Morris pushed his researches farther and brought up words almost pre-Chaucerian. Every language in Europe has been put under contribution at one time or another for one purpose or another. The military vocabulary, for instance, reveals the former superiority of the French, just as the naval vocabulary reveals the former superiority of the Dutch. And as modern science has extended its conquests, it has drawn on Greek for its terms of precision.

Under this influx of foreign words, old and new, the framework of the original London dialect stands solidly enough, but it is visible only to the scholarly specialist in linguistic research. But the latest London dialect, the speech of the inhabitants of the British capital at the end of the nineteenth century, has ceased absolutely to serve as a standard. Whatever utility there was in the past in accepting as normal English the actual living dialect of London has long since departed without a protest. No educated Englishman any longer thinks of conforming his syntax or his vocabulary to the actual living dialect of London, whether of the court or of the slums. Indeed, so far is he from accepting the verbal habits of the man in the street as suggesting a standard for him that he is wont to hold them up to ridicule as cockney corruptions. He likes to laugh at the tricks of speech that he discovers on the lips of the Londoners, at their dropping of their initial *h*'s more often than he deems proper, and at their more recent substitution of *y* for *a*—as in "tyke the cyke, lydy."

The local standard of London has thus been disestablished in the course of the centuries simply because there was no longer a necessity for any local standard. The speech of the capital served as the starting-point of the language; and in the early days a local standard of usage was useful. But now, after English has enjoyed a thousand years of growth, a standard so primitive is not only useless, but it would be very injurious. Nor could any other local standard be substituted for that of London without manifest danger—even if the acceptance of such a standard was possible. The peoples that speak English are now too widely scattered and their needs are too many and too diverse for any local standard not to be retarding in its limitations.

To-day the standard of English is to be sought not in the actual living dialect of the inhabitants of any district or of any country, but in the language itself, in its splendid past and in its mighty present. Five hundred years ago, more or less, Chaucer sent forth the first masterpieces of English literature; and in all those five centuries the language has never lacked poets and prose-writers who knew its secrets and could bring forth its beauties. Each of them has helped to make English what it is now; and a study of what English has been is all that we need to enable us to see what it will be —and what it should be. Any attempt to trammel it by a local standard, or by academic restrictions, or by school-masters' grammar-rules, is certain to fail. In the past, English has shaken itself free of many a limitation; and in the present it is insisting on its own liberty to take the short-cut whenever that enables it to do its work with less waste of time. We cannot doubt that in the future it will go on in its own way, making itself fitter for the manifold needs of an expanding race which has the unusual characteristic of having lofty ideals while being intensely practical. A British poet it was, Lord Houghton, who once sent these prophetic lines to an American lady:

> That ample speech! That subtle speech!
> Apt for the need of all and each;
> Strong to endure, yet prompt to bend

> Wherever human feelings tend.
> Preserve its force; *expand its powers*;
> And through the maze of civic life,
> In Letters, Commerce, even in Strife,
> Forget not it is yours and ours.

The English language is the most valuable possession of the peoples that speak it, and that have for their chief cities, not London alone, or Edinburgh or Dublin, but also New York and Chicago, Calcutta and Bombay, Melbourne and Montreal. The English language is one and indivisible, and we need not fear that the lack of a local standard may lead it ever to break up into fragmentary dialects. There is really no danger now that English will not be uniform in all the four quarters of the world, and that it will not modify itself as occasion serves. We can already detect divergencies of usage and of vocabulary; but these are only trifles. The steamship and the railroad and the telegraph bring the American and the Briton and the Australian closer together nowadays than were the users of the Midland dialect when Chaucer set forth on his pilgrimage to Canterbury; and then there is the printing-press, whereby the newspaper and the school-book and the works of the dead-and-gone masters of our literature bind us together with unbreakable links.

These divergencies of usage and of vocabulary—London from Edinburgh, and New York from Bombay—are but evidences of the healthy activity of our tongue. It is only when it is dead that a language ceases to grow. It needs to be constantly refreshed by new words and phrases as the elder terms are exhausted. Lowell held it to be part of Shakspere's good fortune that he came when English was ripe and yet fresh, when there was an abundance of words ready to his hand, but none of them yet exhausted by hard work. So Mr. Howells has recently recorded his feeling that any one who now employs English "to depict or to characterize finds the phrases thumbed over and worn and blunted with incessant use," and experiences a joy in the bold locutions which are now and again "reported from the lips of the people."

"From the lips of the people";—here is a phrase that would have sadly shocked a narrow-minded scholar like Dr. Johnson. But what the learned of yesterday denied—and, indeed, have denounced as rank heresy—the more learned of to-day acknowledge as a fact. The real language of a people is the spoken word, not the written. Language lives on the tongue and in the ear; there it was born, and there it grows. Man wooed his wife and taught his children and discussed with his neighbors for centuries before he perfected the art of writing. Even to-day the work of the world is done rather by the spoken word than by the written. And those who are doing the work of the world are following the example of our remote ancestors who did not know how to write; when they feel new needs they will make violent efforts to supply those needs, devising fresh words put together in rough-and-ready fashion, often ignorantly. The mouth is ever willing to try verbal experiments, to risk a new locution, to hazard a wrenching of an old term to a novel use. The hand that writes is always slow to accept the result of these attempts to meet a demand in an unauthorized way. The spoken language bristles with innovations, while the written language remains properly conservative. Few of these oral babes are viable, and fewer still survive; while only now and again does one of these verbal foundlings come of age and claim citizenship in literature.

In the antiquated books of rhetoric which our grandfathers handed down to us there are solemn warnings against neologisms—and neologism was a term of reproach designed to stigmatize a new word as such. But in the stimulating study of certain of the laws of linguistics, which M. Bréal, one of the foremost of French philologists, has called 'Semantics,' we are told that to condemn neologisms absolutely would be most unfortunate and most useless. "Every progress in a language is, first of all, the act of an individual, and then of a minority, large or small. A land where all innovation should be forbidden would take from its language all chance of development." And M. Bréal points out that language must keep on transforming itself with every new discovery and invention, with the incessant modification of our manners, of our customs, and even of our ideas. We are all of us at work on the vocabulary of the future, ignorant and learned, authors and artists, the man of the world and the man in the street; and even our children have a share in this labor, and by no means the least.

Among all these countless candidates for literary acceptance, the struggle for existence is very fierce, and only the fittest of the new words survive. Or, to change the figure, conversation might be called the Lower House, where all the verbal coinages must have their origin, while literature is the Upper House, without whose concurrence nothing can be established. And the watch-dogs of the treasury are trustworthy; they resist all attempts of which they do not approve. In language, as in politics, the power of the democratic principle is getting itself more widely acknowledged. The people blunders more often than not, but it knows its own mind; and in the end it has its own way. In language, as in politics, we Americans are really conservative. We are well aware that we have the right to make what change we please, and we know better than to exercise this right. Indeed, we do not desire to do so. We want no more change in our laws or in our language than is absolutely necessary.

We have modified the common language far less than we have modified the common law. We have kept alive here many a word and many a meaning which was well worthy of preservation, and which our kin across the seas had permitted to perish. Professor Earle of Oxford, in his comprehensive volume on 'English Prose,' praises American authors for refreshing old words by novel combinations. When Mr. W. Aldis Wright drew up a glossary of the words, phrases, and constructions in the King James translation of the Bible and in the Book of Common Prayer, which were obsolete in Great Britain in the sense that they would no longer naturally find a place in ordinary prose-writing, Professor Lounsbury pointed out that at least a sixth of these words, phrases, and constructions are not now obsolete in the United States, and would be used by any American writer without fear that he might not be understood. As Lowell said, our ancestors "unhappily could bring over no English better than Shakspere's," and by good fortune we have kept alive some of the Elizabethan boldness of imagery. Even our trivial colloquialisms have often a metaphoric vigor now rarely to be matched in the street-phrases of the city where Shakspere earned his living. Ben Jonson would have relished one New York phrase that an office-holder gives an office-seeker, "the glad hand and the marble heart," and that other which described a former favorite comedian as now having "a fur-lined voice."

When Tocqueville came over here in 1831, he thought that we Americans had already modified the English language. British critics, like Dean Alford, have often animadverted upon the deterioration of the language on this side of the Atlantic. American humorists, like Mark Twain, have calmly claimed that the tongue they used was not English, but American. It is English as Mark Twain uses it, and English of a force and a clarity not surpassed by any living writer of the language; but in so far as American usage differs from British, it was according to the former and not according to the latter. But they differ in reality very slightly indeed; and whatever divergence there may be is rather in the spoken language than in the written. That the spoken language should vary is inevitable and advantageous, since the more variation is attempted, the better opportunity the language has to freshen up its languishing vocabulary and to reinvigorate itself. That the written language should widely vary would be the greatest of misfortunes.

Of this there is now no danger whatever, and never has been. The settlement of the United States took place after the invention of printing; and the printing-press is a sure preventive of a new dialect nowadays. The disestablishment of the local standard of London leaves English free to develop according to its own laws and its own logic. There is no longer any weight of authority to be given to contemporary British usage over contemporary American usage—except in so far as the British branch of English literature is more resplendent with names of high renown than the American branch. That this was the case in the nineteenth century—that the British poets and prose-writers outnumber and outvalue the American—must be admitted at once; that it will be the case throughout the twentieth century may be doubted. And whenever the poets and prose-writers of the American branch of English literature are superior in number and in power to those of the British branch, then there can be no doubt as to where the weight of authority will lie. The shifting of the center of power will take place unconsciously; and the development of English will go on just the same after it takes place as it is going on now. The conservative forces are in no danger of overthrow at the hands of the radicals, whether in the United States or in Great Britain or in any of her colonial dependencies.

Perhaps the principle which will govern can best be stated in another quotation from M. Bréal: "The limit within which the right to innovate stops is not fixed by any idea of 'purity' (which can always be contested); it is fixed by the need we have to keep in contact with the thought of those who have preceded us. The more considerable the literary past of a people, the more this need makes itself felt as a duty, as a condition of dignity and force." And there is no sign that either the American or the British half of those who have our language for a mother-tongue is in danger of becoming disloyal to the literary past of English literature, that most magnificent heritage—the birthright of both of us.

(1899)

IV
THE LANGUAGE IN GREAT BRITAIN

There is a wide gap between the proverb asserting that "figures never lie" and the opinion expressed now and again by experts that nothing can be more mendacious than statistics misapplied; and the truth seems to lie between these extreme sayings. Just as chronology is the backbone of history, so a statement of fact can be made terser and more convincing if the figures are set forth that illuminate it. If we wish to perceive the change of the relative position of Great Britain and the United States in the course of the centuries, nothing can help us better to a firm grasp of the exact facts of the case than a comparison of the population of the two countries at various periods.

In 1700 the inhabitants of Great Britain and Ireland numbered between eight and nine millions, while the inhabitants of what is now the United States were, perhaps, a scant three hundred thousand. In 1900, the people of the British Isles are reckoned at some thirty-seven millions more or less, and the people of the United States are almost exactly twice as many, being about seventy-five millions. To project a statistical curve into the future is an extra-hazardous proceeding; and no man can now guess at the probable population either of the United Kingdom or of the United States in the year 2000; but as the rate of increase is far larger in America than in England, there is little risk in suggesting that a hundred years from now the population of the American republic will be at least four or five times as large as that of the British monarchy.

Just as the center of population of the United States has been steadily working its way westward, having been in 1800 in Maryland and being in 1900 in Indiana, so also the center of population of the English-speaking race has been steadily moving toward the Occident. Just as the first of these has had to cross the Alleghanies during the nineteenth century, so will the second of them have to cross the Atlantic during the twentieth century. Whether this latter change shall take place early in the century or late, is not important; one day or another it will take place, assuredly.

Inevitably it will be accompanied or speedily followed by another change of almost equal significance. London sooner or later will cease to be the literary center of the English-speaking race. For many centuries the town by the Thames has been the heart of English literature; and there are now visible very few signs that the days of its supremacy are numbered. Even in the United States to-day the old colonial attitude, not yet abandoned, causes us Americans often to be as well acquainted with second-rate British authors as the British are with American authors of the first rank. Yet it is not without significance that at the close of the nineteenth century the two most widely known writers of the language should be one of them an American citizen and the other a British colonial, owing no local allegiance to London—Mark Twain and Rudyard Kipling.

The disestablishment of London as the literary center of English will be retarded by various circumstances. Only very reluctantly is a tradition of preëminence overthrown when consecrated by the centuries. The conditions of existence in England are likely long to continue to be more favorable to literary productivity than are the conditions in America. In a new country literature finds an eager rival in life itself, with all its myriad opportunities for self-expression. No paradox is it to say that more than one American bard may have preferred to build his epic in steel or in stone rather than in words. The creative imagination has outlets here denied it in a long-settled community, residing tranquilly in a little island, where even the decorous landscape seems to belong to the Established Church. But the Eastern States are already, many of them, as orderly and as placid as Great Britain has been for a century. The conditions in England and in America are constantly tending toward equalization.

A time will come, and probably long before the close of the twentieth century, when there will be in the United States not only several times as many people as there are in the British Isles, but also far more literary activity. Sooner or later most of the leading authors of English literature will be American and not British in their training, in their thought, in their ideals. That is to say, the British in the middle of the twentieth century will hold to the Americans about the same position that the Americans held toward the British in the middle of the nineteenth century. The group of American authors between 1840 and 1860 contained Irving and Cooper, Emerson and Hawthorne, Longfellow and Lowell, Poe and Whitman and

Thoreau. These are names endeared to us and highly important to us, and not to be neglected in any consideration of English literature; but it is foolish for an American to seek to set them up as the equal of the British group flourishing during the same score of years. So in the middle of the twentieth century the British group will probably not lack striking individualities; but, as a whole, it will probably be surpassed by the American group. The largest portion of the men of letters who use English to express themselves, as well as the largest body of the English-speaking race, will have its residence on the western shore of the Western Ocean.

What will then happen to the English language in England when England awakens to the fact that the center of the English-speaking race is no longer within the borders of the little island? Will the speech of the British sink into dialectic corruption, or will the British resolutely stamp out their undue local divergences from the normal English of the main body of the users of the language in the United States? Will they frankly accept the inevitable? Will they face the facts as they are? Will they follow the lead of the Americans when we shall have the leadership of the language, as the Americans followed their lead when they had it? Or will they insist on an arbitrary independence, which can have only one result—the splitting off of the British branch of our speech from the main stem of the language? To ask these questions is to project an inquiry far into the future, but the speculation is not without an interest of its own. And altho it is difficult to decide so far in advance of the event, yet we have now some of the material on which to base a judgment as to what is likely to happen.

Of course, the question is not one to be answered offhand; and not a few arguments could be brought forward in support of the opinion that the British speech of the future is likely to separate itself from the main body of English as then spoken in this country. In the first place, England, altho it has already ceased to be the most populous of the countries using English, will still be the senior partner of the great trading-company known as the British Empire. That the British Empire may be dissolved is possible, no doubt. The Australian colonies have federated; and having formed a strong union of their own, they may prefer to stand alone. South Africa may follow the example of Australia. India may arise in the might of her millions and cast out its English rulers. Canada may decide to throw in its lot with the greater American republic. But each of these things is improbable; and that they should all come to pass is practically inconceivable. All signs now seem to point not only to a continuance of the British Empire, but also to its steady expansion. London is likely long to be the capital of an empire upon which the sun never sets, an empire inhabited by men of every color and every creed and every language. For these men English must serve as the means of communication one with another, Hindu with Parsee, Boer with Zulu, Chinook with Canuck.

That this will put a strain on the language is indisputable. Wherever any tongue serves as a *lingua franca* for men of various stocks, there is an immediate tendency toward corruption. There is a constant pressure to simplify and to lop off and to reduce to the bare elements. The Pidgin-English of the Chinese coast is an example of what may befall a noble language when it is enslaved to serve many masters, ignorant of its history and careless of its idioms. Mr. Kipling's earliest tales are some of them almost incomprehensible to readers unacquainted with the vocabulary of the competition-walla; and the reports of the British generals during the war with the Boers were besprinkled with words not hitherto supposed to be English.

Some observers see in this a menace to the integrity of the language, a menace likely to become more threatening as the British Empire spreads itself still farther over the waste places of the earth. But is there not also a danger in the integrity of English close at home—in England itself, even in London, and not afar in the remote borders of the Empire—the danger due to the prevalence of local dialects? To the student of language one of the most obvious differences between Great Britain and the United States lies in the fact that we in America have really no local dialects such as are common in England. Every county of England has an indigenous population, whose ancestors dwelt in the same place since a time whereof the memory of man runneth not to the contrary; and this indigenous population has its own peculiarities of pronunciation, of vocabulary, and of idiom, handed down from father to son, generation after generation. But no one of the United States was settled exclusively by immigrants from a single English county; and, therefore, no one of these local dialects was ever transplanted bodily to America. And no considerable part of the United States has a stationary population, inbreeding and stagnant and impervious to outside influences; indeed, to be nomadic, to be here to-day and there to-morrow, to be born in New England, to grow up in the middle west, to be married in New York, and to die in Colorado—is not this a characteristic of us Americans? And it is a characteristic fatal to the development of real dialects in this country such as are abundant in England. Of course we have our local peculiarities of idiom and of pronunciation, but these are very superficial indeed. Probably there has been a closer uniformity of speech throughout the United States for fifty years past than there is even to-day in Great Britain, where the Yorkshireman cannot understand the cockney, and where the Scot sits silent in the house of the Cornishman.

This uniformity of speech throughout the United States is, perhaps, partly the result of Noah Webster's 'Spelling-Book.' It has certainly been aided greatly by the public-school system, firmly established throughout the country, and steadily strengthening itself. The school system of the United Kingdom is younger by far; it is not yet adequately organized; it has still to be adjusted to its place in a proper scheme of national education. In the higher institutions of learning in England, at Oxford and at Cambridge, there is no postgraduate work in English; and whatever instruction an undergraduate may get there in English literature is incidental, not to say accidental.

Probably there is no connection between this lack of university instruction in English and a carelessness in the use of the language which strikes us unpleasantly, not merely in the unpremeditated letters of scholarly Englishmen, but sometimes even in their more academic efforts. Jowett's correspondence, for example, and Matthew Arnold's, offer examples of a slovenliness of phrase not to be found in Lowell's letters or in Emerson's.

Certain Briticisms are very prevalent, not merely among the uneducated, but among the more highly cultivated. *Directly* is used for *as soon as* by Archbishop Trench (the author of a lively little book on words) and by Mr. Courthope (the Oxford professor of poetry). *Like* is used for *as*—that is, "like we do"—by Charles Darwin, and in more than one volume of the English Men of Letters series, edited by Mr. John Morley. The elision of the initial *h*, which the British themselves like to think a test of breeding, is discoverable far more often than they imagine on the lips of those who ought to know better. It is said that Lord Beaconsfield, for example, sometimes dropped his *h*'s, and that he once spoke of "the 'urried 'Udson." And if we may rely on the evidence of spelling, the British often leave the *h* silent where we Americans sound it. They write *an historical essay* from which it is a fair inference that they pronounce the adjective *'istorical*. In Mr. Kipling's 'From Sea to Sea' he writes not only *an hotel* and *an hospital*, but also *an hydraulic*.

Thus we see that the immense size and variegated population of the British Empire may be considered as a menace to the integrity of the English language in the British Isles; and that a second source of danger is to be discovered in the local dialects of Great Britain; and, finally, that there is observable in England even now a carelessness in the use of the language and a willingness to innovate both in vocabulary and in idiom.

But however formidable these three tendencies may look when massed together, there is really no weight to be attached to any of them singly or to all of them combined. The language has already for two centuries been exposed to contact with countless other tongues in America and Asia and Africa without appreciable deterioration up to the present time; and there is no reason to fear that this contact will be more corrupting in the twentieth century than it has been in the nineteenth. On the contrary, it will result rather in an enrichment and refreshment of the vocabulary. The danger from the local dialects of Great Britain, instead of increasing, is decreasing day by day as the facilities for travel improve and as the schoolmaster is able to impose his uniform English upon the young. Lastly, the willingness to use new words not authorized by the past of the language is in itself not blameworthy; it may be indeed commendable when it is restrained by a conservative instinct and controlled by reason.

The Briticisms that besprinkle the columns of London newspapers are like the Americanisms to be seen in the pages of the New York newspapers in that they are evidences of vitality, of the healthiness of the language itself. In Latin it may be proper enough for us to set up a Ciceronian standard and to reject any usage not warranted by the masterly orator; but in English it is absurd to declare any merely personal standard and to reject any term or any idiom because it was unknown to Chaucer or to Shakspere, to Addison or to Franklin, to Thackeray or to Hawthorne. Latin is dead, and the Ciceronian decision as regards the propriety of any usage may be accepted as final. English is a living tongue, and the great writers of every generation make unhesitating use of words and of constructions which the great writers of earlier generations were ignorant of or chose to ignore.

The most of these British innovations, both of to-day and of to-morrow, will be individual and freakish; and, therefore, they will win no foothold even in the British vocabulary. But a few of them will prove their own excuse for being, and these will establish themselves in Great Britain. The best of them, those of which the necessity is indisputable, will spread across the Atlantic and will be welcomed by the main body of users of English over here—just as certain American innovations and revivals were hospitably received in England when only the smaller branch of the English-speaking race was on the American side of the ocean. And, of course, the new terms which spring into existence in the United States after the literary center of the language has crossed the Atlantic will be carried over to England in books and in periodicals.

When the bulk of contemporary English literature is produced by American authors, and when the British themselves have accepted the situation and resigned themselves at last to the departure of the literary supremacy of London, then the weight of American precedent will be overwhelming. Without knowing it, British readers of American books will be led to conform to American usage; and American terms will not seem outlandish to them, as these words and phrases do even now, when comparatively few American authors are read in Great Britain. And these American innovations will be very few, for the conservative instinct is in some ways stronger in the United States than it is in Great Britain, due perhaps partly to the more wide-spread popular education here, which gives to every child a certain solidarity with the past.

It is education and the school-book; it is the printing-press and the newspaper and the magazine; it is the ease of travel across the Atlantic and the swiftness of the voyage;—it is a combination of all these things which will prevent any development of a British branch of the language after the numerical preponderance of the American people becomes overwhelming. And working toward the same union is a loyal conservatism, due in a measure to a proud enjoyment of the great literature of the language, the common possession of both British and Americans, having its past in the keeping of the elder division of the stock, and certain to transfer its future to the care of the younger division.

To declare that the literary center of English is to be transferred sooner or later from the British Isles to the United States may seem to some a hazardous prediction; and yet it is as safe as any prophecy before the event can hope to be. Such a transfer, it is true, is perhaps unprecedented in literary history,—altho the scholar may see a close parallel in the preëminence once attained by Alexandria as the capital of Greek culture. Unprecedented or not, phenomenal or not, the transfer is inevitable sooner or later.

(1899)

V
AMERICANISMS ONCE MORE

It is a reflection upon what we are wont to term a liberal education that the result of college training sometimes appears to be rather a narrowing of the mental outlook than the broadening we have a right to anticipate. What a student ought to have got from his four years of labor is a conviction of the vastness of human knowledge and a proper humility, due to his discovery that he himself possesses only an infinitesimal fraction of the total sum. Many graduates—indeed, most of them nowadays, we may hope —have attained to this much of wisdom: that they are not puffed up by the few things they do know, so much as made modest by the many things they cannot but admit themselves to be ignorant of. With the increasing specialization of the higher education, the attitude of the graduate is likely to be increasingly humble; and a college man will not be led to feel that he is expected to know everything about everything.

Perhaps the disputatious arrogance of a few of the younger graduates of an earlier generation was due to the dogmatism of the teaching they sat under. In nothing is our later instruction more improved than in the disappearance of this authoritative tone—due in great measure, it may be, to the unsettling of old theories by new facts. In no department of learning was the manner more dogmatic than in the teaching of the English language. The older rhetoricians had no doubts at all on the subject. They never hesitated as to the finality of their own judgment on all disputed points. They were sure that they knew just what the English language ought to be; and it never entered into their heads to question their own competence to declare the standard of speech. Yet, as a matter of fact, they knew little of the long history of the language, and they had no insight into the principles that were governing its development. At most, their information was limited to the works of their immediate predecessors; and for a more remote past they had the same supreme contempt they were ever displaying toward the actual present. Thus they were ever ready to lay down rules made up out of their own heads; and their acts were as arbitrary as their attitude was intolerant.

In his 'Philosophy of Rhetoric,' which he tells us was planned in 1750, Dr. George Campbell quotes with approval Dr. Johnson's assertion that the "terms of the laboring and mercantile part of the people" are mere "fugitive cant," not to be "regarded as part of the durable matter of a language." Dr. Campbell himself refuses to consider it as an evidence of reputable and present use that a word or a phrase has been employed by writers of political pamphlets or by speakers in the House of Commons, and he declares that he has selected his prose examples "neither from living authors, nor from those who wrote before the Revolution: not from the first, because an author's fame is not so firmly established in his lifetime; nor from the last, that there may be no suspicion that his style is superannuated." Now contrast this narrow-mindedness with the liberality discoverable in our more recent text-books—in the 'Elements of Rhetoric,' for example, of Professor George R. Carpenter, who tells us frankly that "whenever usage seems to differ, one's own taste and sense must be called into play." Professor Carpenter then pleads "for a considerable degree of tolerance in such matters. If we know what a man means, and if his usage is in accordance with that of a large number of intelligent and educated people, it cannot justly be called incorrect. For language rests, at bottom, on convention or agreement, and what a large body of reputable people recognize as a proper word or a proper meaning of a word cannot be denied its right to a place in the English vocabulary."

For an Englishman to object to an Americanism as such, regardless of its possible propriety or of its probable pertinence, and for an American to object to a Briticism as such—either of these things is equivalent to a refusal to allow the English language to grow. It is to insist that it is good enough now and that it shall not expand in response to future needs. It is to impose on our written speech a fatal rigidity. It is an attempt on the part of pedants so to bind the limbs of the language that a vigorous life will soon be impossible. With all such efforts those who have at heart the real welfare of our tongue will have no sympathy—least of all the strong men of literature who are forever ravenous after new words and old. Victor Hugo, for example, so far back as 1827, when the modern science of linguistics was still in its swaddling-clothes, had no difficulty in declaring the truth. "The

French language," he wrote in the preface to 'Cromwell,' "is not fixed, and it never will be. A living language does not fix itself. Mind is always on the march, or, if you will, in movement, and languages move with it.... In vain do our literary Joshuas command the language to stand still; neither the language nor the sun stands still any more. The day they do they fix themselves; it will be because they are dying. That is why the French of a certain contemporary school is a dead language."

In the 'Art of French Poetry,' first printed in 1565, Ronsard, one of the most adroit of Victor Hugo's predecessors in the mastery of verse, proffers this significant advice to his fellow-craftsmen (I am availing myself of the satisfactory translation of Professor B. W. Wells): "You must choose and appropriate dexterously to your work the most significant words of the dialects of our France, especially if you have not such good or suitable words in your own dialect; and you must not mind whether the words are of Gascony, of Poitiers, of Normandy, Manche, or Lyonnais, as long as they are good and signify exactly what you want to say.... And observe that the Greek language would never have been so rich in dialects or in words had it not been for the great number of republics that flourished at that time, ... whence came many dialects, all held without distinction as good by the learned writers of those times. For a country can never be so perfect in all things that it cannot borrow sometimes from its neighbors."

Here we have Ronsard declaring clearly that local varieties of speech are most useful to the common tongue. Indeed, we may regard the dialect of any district as a cache—a hidden storehouse—at which the language may replenish itself whenever its own supplies are exhausted. Whoever has had occasion to study any of these dialects, whether in Greek or in French or in English, must have been delighted often at the freshness and the force of words and phrases unexpectedly discovered. Edward Fitzgerald, the translator of Omar Khayyam, made an affectionate collection of Suffolk sea-phrases, and from these a dozen might be culled, or a score or more, by the use of which the English language would be the gainer. Lowell's loving and learned analysis of the speech of his fellow New-Englanders is familiar to all readers of the 'Biglow Papers.' It was Lowell also who has left us this brilliant definition: "True Americanisms are self-cocking phrases or words that are wholly of our own make, and do their work shortly and sharply at a pinch."

Characteristically witty this definition is, no doubt, but not wholly adequate. What is an Americanism? And what is a Briticism? Not long ago a friendly British writer rebuked his fellow-countrymen for a double failing of theirs—for their twin tricks of assuming, first, that every vulgarism unfamiliar to them is an Americanism, and that therefore, and secondly, every Americanism is a vulgarism. In the mouths of many British speakers "Americanism" serves as a term of reproach; and so does "Briticism" in the mouths of some American speakers. But this should not be; the words ought to be used with scientific precision and with no flush of feeling. Before using them, we must ascertain with what exact meaning it is best to employ them.

An American investigator gathered together a dozen or two queer words and phrases that he had noted in recent British books and journals, and as they were then wholly unknown to America, he branded them as Briticisms, only to evoke a prompt protest from Mr. Andrew Lang. For the stigmatized words and phrases Mr. Lang proffered no defense; but he boldly denied that it was fair to call them Briticisms. True, one or another of them had been detected in pages of this or that British author. Yet they were not common property: they were individualisms; they were to be charged against each separate perpetrator and not against the whole United Kingdom. Mr. Lang maintained that when Walter Pater used so odd a term as *evanescing*, this use "scarcely makes it a Briticism; it was a Paterism."

This is a plea in confession and avoidance, but its force is indisputable. To admit it, however, gives us a right to insist that the same justice shall be meted out to the so-called Americanisms which Mr. Lang has more than once held up to British execration. If the use of an ill-made word like *essayette* or *leaderette* or *sermonette* by one or more British writers does not make it a Briticism until it can be proved to have come into general use in Great Britain, then, of course, the verbal aberrations of careless Americans, or even the freakish dislocations of the vocabulary indulged in by some of our more acrobatic humorists, does not warrant a British writer in calling any chance phrase of theirs an Americanism. Mr. W. S. Gilbert once manufactured the verb "to burgle," and Mr. Gilbert is a British writer of good repute; but *burgling* is not therefore a Briticism: it is a Gilbertism. Mr. Edison, an inventor of another sort, once affirmed that a certain article giving an account of his kineto-phonograph had his "entire indorsation."

According to Mr. Lang's theory, *indorsation*, not being in use generally in the United States, is not an Americanism: it is an Edisonism.

The more Mr. Lang's theory is considered, the sounder it will appear. Individual word-coinages are not redeemable at the national treasury either in the United Kingdom or in the United States. Before a word or a phrase can properly be called a Briticism or an Americanism there must be proof that it has won its way into general use on its own side of the Atlantic. *Right away* for "at once" is an Americanism beyond all dispute, for it is widespread throughout the United States; and so is *back of* for "behind." *Directly* for "as soon as" is a Briticism equally indisputable; and so is *different to* for "different from." In each of these four cases there has been a local divergence from the traditional usage of the English language. All four of these divergences may be advantageous, and all four of them may even be accepted hereafter on both sides of the Atlantic; but just now there is no doubt that two of them are fairly to be called Americanisms and two of them are properly to be recorded as Briticisms.

Every student of our speech knows that true Americanisms are abundant enough; but the omission of terms casually employed here and there, seed that fell by the wayside, springing up only to wilt away—the omission of all individualisms of this sort simplifies the list immensely, just as a like course of action in England cuts down the number of Briticisms fairly to be catalogued as such. It must be remarked, however, that the collecting of so-called Americanisms is a pastime that has been carried on since the early years of the nineteenth century, whereas it was only in the closing decades of that century that attention was called to the existence of Briticisms, and to the necessity of a careful collection of them. The bulky tomes which pretend to be 'Dictionaries of Americanisms' are stuffed with words and phrases having no right there.

These dictionaries would be very slim if they contained only true Americanisms, that is to say, words and phrases in common use in the United States and not in common use in the United Kingdom. Yet they would be slimmer still if another limitation is imposed on the use of the word. Is a term fairly to be called an Americanism if it can be shown to have been formerly in use in England, even though it may there have dropped out of sight in the past century or two? Now, everybody knows that dozens of so-called Americanisms are good old English, neglected by the

British and allowed to die out over there, but cherished and kept alive over here. Such is *guess*="incline to think"; such is *realise*="to make certain or substantial"; such is *reckon*="consider" or "deem"; such is *a few*="a little"; such is *nights*="at night"; and such are dozens of other words often foolishly animadverted upon as indefensible Americanisms, and all of them solidly established in honorable ancestry. An instructive collection of these survivals can be seen in Mr. H. C. Lodge's aptly entitled and highly interesting essay on 'Shakspere's Americanisms.'

It is with an amused surprise that an American in his occasional reading keeps coming across in the pages of British authors of one century or another what he had supposed to be Americanisms, and even what he had taken sometimes for mere slang. The *cert* of the New York street-boy, apparently a contraction of *certainly*, is it not rather the *certes* of the Elizabethans? And the interrogative *how?*="what is it?"—a usage abhorred by Dr. Holmes,—this can be discovered in Massinger's plays more than once ('Duke of Milan,' iii. 3, and 'Believe as You List,' ii. 2). "I'm *pretty considerably* glad to see you," says Manuel, in Colley Cibber's 'She Would and She Would Not.' *To fire out*="expel forcibly," is in Shakspere's Sonnets and also in 'Ralph Roister Doister'—altho, perhaps, with a slightly different connotation from that now obtaining in America. A theatrical manager nowadays likes to have the first performance of a new play out of town so that he can come to the metropolis with a perfected work, and he calls this *trying it on the dog*; the same expression, almost, is to be found in Pope. In 'Pickwick,' Sam Weller proposes to *settle the hash* of an opponent; and in 'Tess of the d'Urbervilles' we find *down to the ground* used as a superlative, and quite in our own later sense. The Southern *peart* is in 'Lorna Doone,' and the Southwestern *dog-gone it* is in the 'Little Minister.' In Mr. Barrie's story also do we find *to go back on your word*; just as in Mr. William Watson's 'Excursions in Criticism' we discover *grit*="staying power" or "doggedness."

Very amusing indeed is the attitude of the ordinary British newspaper reviewer toward words and phrases in this category. Not being a scholar in English, he is unaware that scholarship is a condition precedent to judgment; and he is swift to denounce as American innovations terms firmly rooted in the earlier masters of the language, while he passes the frequent Briticisms in the pages of contemporary London writers without a hint of reproof. From a British author like Rossetti he accepts "the *gracile* spring," while he rejects "*gracile* ease" in an American author like Mr. Howells. Behind this arrogant ignorance is to be perceived the assumption that the English language is in immediate peril of disease and death from American license if British newspapers fail to do their duty. The shriller the shriek of protest is, the slighter the protester's competence upon the question at issue. No outcry against the deterioration of English in America has come from any of the British scholars who can speak with authority about the language.

What we Americans have done is to keep alive or to revive many a good old English term; and for this service to our common speech our British cousins ought to be properly grateful. We must admit that words and phrases and usages thus reinstated are not true Americanisms—however much we might like to claim them for our very own. We have already seen that most of the individualisms of eccentric or careless writers are also not to be received as true Americanisms. And there is yet a third group of so-called Americanisms not fairly entitled to the name. These are the terms devised in the United States to meet conditions unknown in England. Here is no divergence from the accepted usage of the language, but a development of the common tongue to satisfy a new necessity. The need for the new word or phrase was first felt in America, and here the new term had to be found to supply the immediate want. But the word itself, altho frankly of American origin, is not to be styled an Americanism. It is a new English word, that is all—a word to be used hereafter in the United Kingdom as in the United States. It is an American contribution to the English language; but it is not an Americanism—if we limit Americanism to mean a term having currency only in North America, just as Briticism means a term having currency only in the British Islands. The new thing exists now, and as it came into existence in America, we stood sponsors for it; but the name we gave it is its name once for all, to be used by the British and the Australians and the Canadians as well as by ourselves. *Telephone,* for example,—both the thing and the word are of American invention,—is there any one so foolish as to call *telephone* an Americanism?

These American contributions to the English language are not a few. Some of them are brand-new words, minted at the minute of sudden demand, and well made or ill made, as chance would have it; *phonograph* is one of these; *dime* is another; and *typewriter* is a third. Some of them are old words wrenched to a new use, like *elevator*="storehouse for grain," and like *ticker*="telegraphic printing-machine." Some of them are taken from foreign tongues, either translated, like *statehouse* (from the Dutch), or unchanged, like *prairie* (from the French), *adobe* (from the Spanish), and *stoop* (from the Dutch). Some of them are borrowed from the rude tongues of our predecessors on this continent, like *moccasin* and *tomahawk* and *wigwam*. To be compared with this last group are the words adopted into English from the native languages of India—*punka*, for example. And I make no doubt that the Australians have taken over from the aborigines round about them more than one word needed in a hurry as a name for something until then nameless in our common language because the something itself was until then unknown or unnoticed. But these Australian contributions to English cannot be called Australianisms any more than *telephone* and *prairie* and *wigwam* can be called Americanisms.

So far the attempt has been here made to subtract from the immense and heterogeneous mass of so-called Americanisms three classes of terms falsely so called: first, the mere individualisms, for which America as a whole has a right to shirk the responsibility; second, the survivals in the United States of words and usages that happen to have fallen into abeyance in Great Britain; and, third, the American contributions to the English language. As to each of these three groups the case is clear enough; but as to a fourth group, which ought also to be deducted, one cannot speak with quite so much confidence.

This group would include the peculiarities of speech existing sporadically in this or that special locality and contributing what are often called the American dialects—the Yankee dialect first of all, then the dialect of the Appalachian mountaineers, the dialect of the Western cow-boys, etc. Are these localisms fairly to be classed as Americanisms? The question, so far as I know, has never been raised before, for it has been taken for granted that if any such things as Americanisms existed at all, they could surely be collected from the mouth of Hosea Biglow. And yet if we pause to think, we cannot but admit that the so-called Yankee dialect is local, that it is unknown outside of New England, and that a majority of the inhabitants of the United States find it almost as strange in their ears as the broad Scotch of Burns. As for the so-called dialect of the cow-boy, it is not a true dialect at all; it is simply carelessly colloquial English with a heavy infusion of fugitive slang; and whatever it may be in itself, it is local to the cow-country. The Appalachian dialect is perhaps more like a true dialect; but it is even less wide-spread than either of the others here picked out for consideration. No one of these three alleged dialects is in any sense national; all three of them are narrowly local—altho the New England speech has spread more or less into the middle west.

Perhaps some light on this puzzle may be had by considering how they regard a similar problem in England itself. The local dialects which still abound throughout the British Isles are under investigation, each by itself. No one has ever suggested the lumping of them all together as Briticisms. Indeed, the very definition of Briticism would debar this. What is a Briticism but a term frequently used throughout Great Britain and not accepted in the United States? And if this definition is acceptable, we are forced to declare that an Americanism is a term frequently used throughout the United States and not accepted in Great Britain. The terms of the Yankee dialect, of the Appalachian, and of the cow-boy, are localisms; they are not frequently used throughout the United States; they are not to be classed as Americanisms any more than the cockney idioms, the Wessex words, and the Yorkshire phrases are to be classed as Briticisms.

It is greatly to be regretted that Dr. Murray and Mr. Bradley and the other editors of the comprehensive Oxford Dictionary have not been so careful as they might be in identifying the locality of American dialectic peculiarities. They have taken great pains to record and circumscribe British dialectic peculiarities; but they are in the habit of appending a vague and misleading (U. S.) to such American words and usages as they may set down. It is to be hoped that they may hereafter aim at a greater exactness in their attributions, since their present practice is quite misleading, as it often suggests that a term is a true Americanism, used freely throughout the United States, when it is perhaps merely an individualism or at best a localism.

Of true Americanisms there are not so very many left, when we have ousted from their usurped places these four groups of terms having no real title to the honorable name. And true Americanisms might be subdivided again into two groups, the one containing the American terms for which there are equivalent Briticisms, thus indicating a divergence of usage, and the other including only the words and phrases which have sprung up here without correlative activity on the other side of the Atlantic.

When the attempt is made to set up parallel columns of Briticisms and Americanisms, each more or less equal to the other, it is with surprise that we discover how few of these equivalencies there are. In other words, the variations of usage between Great Britain and the United States are infrequent. In England the railway was preceded by the stage-coach, and in America the railroad was preceded rather by the river steamboat; and probably this accounts for the slight differentiation observable in the vocabulary of the traveler. But this is not the reason why we in America make misuse of a French word, *dépôt*, while the British prefer the Latin word *terminus*,—restricting its application accurately to the terminal station of a line. In England they name him a *guard* whom we in America name *brakeman* or *trainman*; and it is to be noted that when Stevenson was an Amateur Emigrant he sought to use the word of the country and so mentions the *brakesman*—thus proving again the difficulty of attaining exactness in local usage. The British call that a *goods-train* which we call a *freight-train*; and they speak of a *crossing-plate* when they mean what we know as a *frog*. In the United States a *sleeping-car* is often termed a *sleeper*, whereas in Great Britain what they call a *sleeper* is what we here call a *tie*. They say a *keyless watch* where we say a *stem-winder*. They say *leader* where we say *editorial*. They call that a *lift* which we call an *elevator*; and we call him a *farm-hand* whom they call an *agricultural laborer*. They have even borrowed one Americanism, *caucus*, and made it a Briticism by changing its meaning to signify what we are wont to describe as the *machine* or the *organisation*. It is to be noted also that *corn* in England refers to *wheat* and in America to *maize*; and that in Great Britain *calico* is a plain cotton cloth and in the United States a printed cotton cloth.

This list of correlative Americanisms and Briticisms might be extended, of course; but however sweeping our investigations may be we cannot make it very long. Far longer is the list of American words and phrases and usages for which there is no British equivalent—far too long, indeed, for inclusion in this essay. All that can be done here and now is to pick up a surface specimen or two from the outcroppings to show the quality of the vein. For instance, the vocabulary of the university is largely indigenous—altho we have recently borrowed a British vulgarism, speaking now of the *varsity team* and the *varsity crew*. *Campus* seems to be unknown to the British, and so does *sophomoric*, a most useful epithet understood at once all over the United States. Its absence from the British vocabulary is probably due to the fact that the four-year course of the old-fashioned American college is unknown in England, where there are *freshmen* indeed, but no *sophomores*.

Going out from the academic groves to the open air of the wider West, as so many of our college graduates do every year, we meet with a host of Americanisms vigorous with the free life of the great river and of the grand mountains. But is *blaze*="to mark a trail through the woods by chipping off bits of bark"—is this a true Americanism? Is it not rather an American contribution to the English language? Surely every man in Africa or in Asia who wishes to retrace his path through a virgin forest must needs *blaze* his way as he goes. But *shack*="a cabin of logs driven perpendicularly into the ground"—this is a true Americanism undoubtedly. And its compound *claim-shack*="a shack built to hold a claim on a preëmption"—this is another true Americanism likely to puzzle a British reader. Even *preëmpt* and *preëmption* are probably Americanisms in that they have with us a meaning somewhat different from that they may have on the other side of the Atlantic. Another true Americanism, which comes to us from the plains, is *mavericks*="the unbranded cattle at large to become the property of the first ranch-owner whose men may chance upon them." And *ranch*, while it is itself a contribution to the language, has usages in which it is an Americanism merely—as in the Californian *hen-ranch*, for example.

There is a large freedom about the Western vernacular and a swift directness not elsewhere observable in the English language, whether in the United States or in the British Empire. These are most valuable qualities, and they are likely to be of real service to English in helping to refresh the jaded vocabulary of more scholarly communities. The function of slang as a true feeder of language is certain to get itself more widely recognized as time goes on; and there is no better nursery for these seedlings of speech than the territory west of the Mississippi and east of the Rockies. To say this is not to say that there are not to be found east of the Mississippi many interesting locutions still inadequately established in the language. For example, there are three words applied to the same thing in different parts of the East; perhaps they ought to be styled localisms, but as they would be comprehended all over the United States, they are probably entitled to be received as true Americanisms—if, on the other hand, they are not in fact good old English words. A pass through the hills is often called a *notch* in the White Mountains, a *clove* in the Catskills, and a *gap* in the Blue Ridge. Yet even as I write this I have my doubts as to there being any narrow geographical delimitation of usage, since I can recall a Parker Notch in the Catskills, not far from Stony Clove and Kaaterskill Clove.

One of the best known of true Americanisms is *lumber*="timber." When we speak of the *lumbering* industry we mean not only the cutting down of trees and their sawing up into planks, but also their marketing. From the apparent participle *lumbering* a verb has been made *to lumber*—a not uncommon process in the history of the language, one British analog being the making of the verb *to bant* from the innocent name of Mr. Banting. *To lumber* is apparently now used in the sense of *to deforest*, if we may rely on a newspaper paragraph which informed us that a certain tract of twenty-five thousand acres in the Adirondacks had "been lumbered, but not in such a way as to injure it for a park." The verb *to launder*="to wash," has been revived of late in America, if indeed it has not been made anew from the noun *laundry*; and shirt-makers in their price-lists specify whether the shirts are to be sold *laundered* or *unlaundered*. And to the word *laundry* itself has been given a further extension of meaning. In New York, at least,—and the verbal fashions of the metropolis spread swiftly throughout the Union,—it signifies not only the place where personal linen is washed but the personal linen itself. An advertisement in a college magazine informed the lone student that "gentlemen's *laundry*" was "mended free."

When an American student of English printed a collection of Briticisms in which more than one strange wild fowl of speech had been snared on the wing in newspapers and advertisements, Mr. Andrew Lang protested against the acceptance of phrases so gathered as representative Briticisms; and it is only fair to admit that they represented colloquial or industrial rather than literary usage. Yet they were interesting in that they gave us a glimpse of the actual speech of the common people—just such a glimpse, in fact, as we get from the Roman inscriptions. This actual speech of the people, whether in Rome or in London or in New York, is the real language, of which the literary dialect is but a sublimation. Language is born in the mouth, altho it dies young unless it is brought up by hand. Language is made sometimes in the library, it is true, and in the parlor also, but far more often in the workshop and on the sidewalk; and nowadays the newspaper and the advertisement record for us the simple and unstilted phrases of the workshop and the sidewalk.

The most of these will fade out of sight unregretted; but a few will prove themselves possessed of sturdy vitality. Briticisms, it may be, or Americanisms, as it happens, they will fight their way up from the workshop to the library, from the sidewalk to the study. Born in a single city, they will serve usefully throughout a great nation, and perhaps in the end all over the world, wherever our language is spoken.

The ideal of style, so it has been tersely put, is the speech of the people in the mouth of the scholar. One reason why so much of the academic writing of educated men is arid is because it is as remote as may be from the speech of the people. One reason why Mark Twain and Rudyard Kipling are now the best-beloved authors of the English language is because they have each of them a welcome ear for the speech of the people. Mark Twain abounds in true Americanisms; on the other hand, Rudyard Kipling is sparing of real Briticisms—having, indeed, a certain hankering after Americanisms. Kipling's case is not unlike that of Æschylus, who was a native of Greece but a frequent resident in Sicily, and in whose vocabulary occasional Sicilianisms have been found by the keen-eyed German critics. So Plautus greedily availed himself of the vigorous fertility he discovered in the vocabulary of the Roman populace; and when Cicero went to the works of Plautus for the words he needed, we had once more the speech of the people in the mouth of the scholar.

Something of the toploftiness of the elder rhetoricians yet lingers in the tone many British writers of to-day see fit to adopt whenever they take occasion to discuss the use of the English language here in America. A trenchant critic like Mr. Frederic Harrison, in a lecture on the masters of style, went out of his way to warn his hearers that though they might be familiar in their writing they were by no means to be vulgar. "At any rate, be easy, colloquial if you like, but shun those vocables which come to us across the Atlantic, or from Newmarket and Whitechapel." This linking of America and Whitechapel may seem to us to be rather vulgar than familiar; and it was Goethe—a master of style well known to Mr. Harrison—who reminded us that "when self-esteem expresses itself in contempt of another, be he the meanest, it must be repellant." It is only fair to say that fewer British writers than ever before sink to so low a level as this; and it is right to admit that a definite recognition of the American joint-ownership of the English language is not now so rare as once it was in England.

Not often, however, do we find so frank and ungrudging acknowledgment of the exact truth as is to be found in Mr. William Archer's 'America To-day.' Part of one of the Scotch critic's paragraphs calls for quotation here because it sets forth, perhaps more clearly and concisely than any American has yet dared to do, what the facts of the case really are:

"There can be no rational doubt, I think, that the English language has gained, and is gaining, enormously by its expansion over the American continent. The prime function of a language, after all, is to interpret the 'form and pressure' of life—the experience, knowledge, thought, emotion, and aspiration of the race which employs it. This being so, the more taproots a language sends down into the soil of life, and the more varied the strata of human experience from which it draws its nourishment, whether of vocabulary or idiom, the more perfect will be its potentialities as a medium of expression. We must be careful, it is true, to keep the organism healthy, to guard against disintegration of tissue; but to that duty American writers are quite as keenly alive as we. It is not a source of weakness but of power and vitality to the English language that it should embrace a greater variety of dialects than any other civilized tongue. A new language, says the proverb, is a new sense; but a multiplicity of dialects means, for the possessors of the main language, an enlargement of the pleasures of the linguistic sense without the fatigue of learning a totally new grammar and vocabulary. So long as there is a potent literary tradition keeping the core of the language one and indivisible, vernacular variations can only tend, in virtue of the survival of the fittest, to promote the abundance, suppleness, and nicety of adaptation of the language as a literary instrument. The English language is no mere historic monument, like Westminster Abbey, to be religiously preserved as a relic of the past, and revered as the burial-place of a bygone breed of giants. It is a living organism, ceaselessly busied, like any other organism, in the processes of assimilation and excretion."

(1899)

VI
NEW WORDS AND OLD

Not long before the opening of the splendid exhibition which, for the short space of six months, made Chicago the most interesting city in the world, its leading literary journal editorially rejoiced that English was becoming a world-language, but sorrowed also that it was sadly in danger of corruption, especially from the piebald jargon of our so-called dialect stories. Not long before the celebration of the Diamond Jubilee of Queen Victoria a notorious sensation-monger of London, having founded a review in which to exploit himself, proclaimed that English was in a parlous state, and that something ought to be done at once or the language would surely die. The Chicago editor was grieved at the sorry condition of our language in the United States, while the London editor wept over its wretched plight in Great Britain. The American journalist called upon us to take pattern by the British; and the British journalist cried out for an Academy like that of the French to lay down laws for the speaking of our mother-tongue—intending perhaps to propose later the revival of the pillory or of the ducking-stool for those who shall infringe the stringent provisions of the new code.

There is nothing novel in these shrill outbreaks, which serve only to alarm the timid and to reveal an unhesitating ignorance of the history of our language. The same kind of protest has been made constantly ever since English has been recognized as a tongue worthy of preservation and protection; and it would be easy to supply parallels without number, some of them five hundred years old. A single example will probably suffice. In Steele's 'Tatler' Swift wrote a letter denouncing "the deplorable ignorance that for some years hath reigned among our English writers, the great depravity of our taste, and the continual corruption of our style." Here we find the 'Tatler' (of London) in the first decade of the eighteenth century saying exactly what the 'Dial' (of Chicago) echoed in the last decade of the nineteenth. But the earlier writer had an excuse the later writer was without; Swift wrote before the history of our language was understood.

We know now that growth is a condition of life; and that only a dead language is rigid. We know now that it is dangerous to elevate the literary diction too far above the speech of the plain people. We have found out that nobody in Rome ever spoke Ciceronian Latin; Cicero did not speak it himself; he did not even write it naturally; he wrote it with an effort and not always to his own satisfaction at the first attempt. We have discovered that there was a wide gap between the elegance of the orator's polished periods and the uncouth bluntness of the vulgar tongue of the Roman people; and we believe that this divergence was broader than that between the perfect style of Hawthorne, for example, and the every-day dialect of Salem or of Concord.

By experts like Whitney we are told that there has been less structural modification of our language in the second half of the nineteenth century than in any other fifty-year period of its existence. Our vocabulary has been enormously enriched, but the skeleton of our speech has been only a little developed. With the decrease in illiteracy the conserving force of the printing-press must always hereafter make change increasingly difficult—even in the obvious cases where improvement is possible. The indirect influence of the novelist and the direct influence of the schoolmaster—very powerful each of them and almost irresistible when united—will always be exerted on the side of the conservatives. To seize these facts firmly and to understand their applications is to have ready always an ample answer for all those who chatter about the impending corruption of our noble tongue.

But we may go further. The study of history shows us that the future of English is dependent not on the watchfulness of its guardians, not upon the increasing richness and flexibility of its vocabulary, not upon the modification of its syntax, not upon the needed reform of its orthography; it is not dependent upon any purity or any corruption of the language itself. The future of the English language is dependent upon the future of the two great peoples that speak it; it is dependent upon the strength, the energy, the vigor, and the virtue of the British and the Americans. A language is but the instrument of those who use it; and English has flourished and spread not because of its own merits, many as they are, but because of the forthputting qualities of the masterful English stock. It must rise and fall with us who speak it. "No speech can do more than express the ideas of those who employ it at the time," so a recent historian of our language has reminded us. "It cannot live upon its past meanings, or upon the past conceptions of great men that have been recorded in it, any more than the race which uses it can live upon its past glory or its past achievements."

When we have once possessed ourselves of the inexorable fact that it is not in our power to warp the development of our language by any conscious effort, we can listen with amused toleration to the excited outcries of those who are constantly protesting against this or that word or phrase or usage which may seem to them new and therefore unjustifiable. We discover also that the self-appointed legislators who lay down the law thus peremptorily are often emphatic in exact proportion to their ignorance of the history of the language.

"Every word we speak," so Dr. Holmes told us, "is the medal of a dead thought or feeling, struck in the die of some human experience, worn smooth by innumerable contacts, and always transferred warm from one to another." We must admit that these chance medalists of language have not always been gifted artists or skilled craftsmen, so the words of their striking are sometimes misshapen; nor have they always respected the standard, so there is counterfeit coin in circulation sometimes. Even when the word is sterling and well minted, be it new or old,

> Now stamped with the image of Good Queen Bess,
>   And now of a Bloody Mary,

the coin itself is sometimes locked up in the reserve, to be misrepresented by a shabby paper promise to pay. So fierce is the popular demand for an increased *per capita* that the verbal currency is ever in danger of debasement. This is the apparent justification of the self-appointed tellers who busy themselves with touchstones of their own and who venture to throw out much false coin. Their tests are trustworthy now and again; but more often than not the pieces they have nailed to the counter are of full weight and ought to pass current.

"There is a purism," Whitney said, "which, while it seeks to maintain the integrity of the language, in effect stifles its growth; to be too fearful of new words and phrases, new meanings, familiar and colloquial expressions, is little less fatal to the well-being of a spoken tongue than to rush into the opposite extreme." And Professor Lounsbury goes further and asserts that our language is not to-day in danger from the agencies commonly supposed to be corrupting it, but rather "from ignorant efforts made to preserve what is called its purity." And elsewhere the same inexpugnable authority reminds us that "the history of language is the history of corruptions," and that "the purest of speakers uses every day, with perfect propriety, words and forms which, looked at from the point of view of the past, are improper, if not scandalous."

There would be both interest and instruction in a list of the many words securely intrenched in our own vocabulary to-day which were bitterly assaulted on their first appearance. Swift praises himself for his valiant effort against certain of these intruders: "I have done my utmost for some years past to stop the progress of *mob* and *banter*, but have been plainly borne down by numbers and betrayed by those who promised to assist me." Puttenham (or whoever it was that wrote the anonymous 'Arte of English Poesie,' published in 1589) admitted the need of certain words to which the purists might justly object, and then adds that "many other like words borrowed out of the Latin and French were not so well to be allowed by us," citing then, among those of which he disapproved, *audacious*, *egregious*, and *compatible*. In the 'Poetaster,' acted in 1601, Ben Jonson satirized Marston's verbal innovations, and among the words he reviled are *clumsy*, *inflate*, *spurious*, *conscious*, *strenuous*, *defunct*, *retrograde*, and *reciprocal*; and in his 'Discoveries' Jonson shrewdly remarked that "a man coins not a new word without some peril and less fruit; for if it happen to be received, the praise is but moderate; if refused, the scorn is assured."

Puttenham wrote at the end of the sixteenth century, Jonson at the beginning of the seventeenth, Swift at the beginning of the eighteenth; and at the beginning of the nineteenth we find Lady Holland declaring *influential* to be a detestable word and asserting that she had tried in vain to get Sheridan to forego it.

At the end of the nineteenth century the battle was still raging over *standpoint*, for example, and over *reliable* and over *lengthy*, and over a score of others, all of which bid fair to establish themselves ultimately because they supply a demand more or less insistent. The fate is more doubtful of *photo* for *photograph* and of *phone* for *telephone*; they both strike us now as vulgarisms, just as *mob* (and for the same reason) struck Swift as vulgar; and it may be that in time they will live down this stigma of illegitimacy just as *mob* has survived it. Then there is the misbegotten verb, *to enthuse,* in my sight the most hideous of vocables. What is to be its fate? Altho I have detected it in the careful columns of the 'Nation,' it has not as yet been adopted by any acknowledged master of English; none the less, I fear me greatly, it has all the vitality of other ill weeds. And is *bike* going to get itself recognized as a substitute for *bicycle,* both as verb and as noun? It seems to be possible, since a monosyllable has always an advantage over a trisyllable in our impatient mouths.

Swift objected sharply to the curtailing of words "when we are already overloaded with monosyllables, which are the disgrace of our language." Then he wittily characterizes the process by which *mob* had been made, *cab* was to be made, and *photo* is now in the making: "Thus we cram one syllable and cut off the rest, as the owl fattened her mice after she had bit off their legs to prevent them from running away; and if ours be the same reason for maiming our words, it will certainly answer the end: for I am sure no other nation will desire to borrow them." Swift was rash enough to assert that *speculation, operation, preliminaries, ambassador, communication,* and *battalion* were words newly introduced, and also to prophesy that they were too poly-syllabic to be able to endure many more campaigns. As it happens no attempt has been made to shorten any one of them except *speculation,* and it can hardly be maintained that *spec* has established itself. Certainly it has not disestablished *speculation,* as *mob* has driven out *mobile vulgus.*

Dryden declared that he traded "both with the living and the dead for the enrichment of our native language"; but he denied that he Latinized too much; and most of the Gallicisms he attempted have not won acceptance. Lowell thought that Dryden did not add a single word to the language, unless "he first used *magnetism* in its present sense of moral attraction." Dr. Holmes also discovered that it is not enough to make a new word when it is needed and to fashion it fitly; its fortune still depends on public caprice or popular instinct. "I've sometimes made new words," he told a friend; "I made *chrysocracy,* thinking it would take its place, but it didn't; *plutocracy,* meaning the same thing, was adopted instead." But *anesthesia* is a word of Dr. Holmes's making which has won its way not only in English but in most of the other modern languages. It may be doubted whether a like fortune will follow another word to be found quoted in one of his letters, *aproposity,* a bilingual hybrid not without analogues in our language.

It is with surprise that in Stevenson's very Scotch romance 'David Balfour' we happen upon another malformation—*come-at-able*, hitherto supposed to be Yankee in its origin and in its aroma. Elsewhere in the same story we read "you *claim* to be innocent," a form which the cockney critics are wont to call American. Stevenson in this novel uses both the modern *jeopardize* and the ancient *enjeopardy*. Just why *to jeopardize* should have driven *to jeopard* out of use, it is not easy to declare, nor why *leniency* is supplanting *lenity*. As *drunk* seems to suggest total intoxication, it is possible to discover the cause of the increasing tendency to say "I have *drank*." No defense is easy of *in our midst* for *in the midst of us*, and yet it will prevail inevitably, for it is a convenient short-cut. Dr. Holmes confessed to Richard Grant White that he had used it once, and that Edward Everett (who had also once fallen from grace) made him see the error of his ways. It is to be found twice in Stevenson's 'Amateur Emigrant,' and again in the 'Res Judicatæ' of Mr. Augustine Birrell, a brisk essayist, altho not an impeccable stylist.

It is nothing against a noun that it is new. To call it a neologism is but begging the question. Of necessity every word was new once. It was "struck in the die of human experience," to come back to Dr. Holmes's figure; and it is at its best before it is "worn smooth by innumerable contacts." Lowell thought it was a chief element of Shakspere's greatness that "he found words ready to his use, original and untarnished—types of thought whose sharp edges were unworn by repeated impressions." He "found a language already established but not yet fetlocked by dictionary and grammar mongers." For the same reason Mérimée delighted in Russian, because it was "young, the pedants not having had time to spoil it; it is admirably fit for poetry."

This native relish for the uncontaminated word it was that led Hugo and Gautier to ransack all sorts of special vocabularies. This thirst for the unhackneyed epithet it is that urges Mr. Rudyard Kipling to avail himself of the technical terms of trade, which serve his purpose, not merely because they are exact, but also because they are unexpected. The device is dangerous, no doubt, but a writer of delicate perceptions can find his advantage in it. Perhaps George Eliot was a little too fond of injecting into fiction the terminology of science, but there was nothing blameworthy in the desire to enlarge the vocabulary which should be at the command of the novelist. Professor Dowden records that when she used in a story words and phrases like *dynamic* and *natural selection,* the reviewer pricked up his delicate ears and shied; and he makes bold to suggest that "if the thoroughbred critic could only be led close up to *dynamic,* he would find that *dynamic* would not bite." Every lover of our language will sympathize with Professor Dowden's assertion that "a protest of common sense is really called for against the affectation which professes to find obscurity in words because they are trisyllabic or because they carry with them scientific associations. Language, the instrument of literary art, is an instrument of ever-extending range, and the truest pedantry, in an age when the air is saturated with scientific thought, would be to reject those accessions to the language which are the special gain of the time."

Where George Eliot erred—if err she did at all in this matter—was in the use of scientific terms inappropriately, or, so to say, boastfully, whereby she aroused an association of ideas foreign to the purpose in hand. Every writer needs to consider most carefully both the obvious and the remote associations of the phrases he employs, that these may intensify the thought he wishes to convey. A word is known by the company it has kept. Especially must a poet have a keen nose for the fragrant word, or else his stanzas will lack savor. The magic of his art lies largely in the syllables he selects, in their sound and in their color. Not their meanings merely are important to him, but their suggestions also—not what they denote more than what they connote. An American psychologist has recently told us that every word has not only its own note but also its overtones. With unconscious foresight, the great poets have always acted on this theory.

Perhaps this is a reason why the poets have ever been ready to rescue a cast-off word from the rubbish-heap of the past. Professor Earle (of Oxford) declares that "it has been one of the most interesting features of the new vigor and independence of American literature, that it has often displayed in a surprising manner what springs of novelty there are in reserve and to be elicited by novel combinations"—a statement more complimentary in its intent than felicitous in its phrasing. And Professor Earle praises Emerson and Lowell and Holmes for their skill in enriching our modern English with the old words locked up out of sight in the treasuries of the past. Lowell said of Emerson that "his eye for a fine, telling phrase that will carry true is like that of a backwoodsman for a rifle; and he will dredge you up a choice word from the mud of Cotton Mather himself."

Of course this effort to recover the scattered pearls of speech, dropped by the wayside in the course of the centuries, is peculiar neither to the United States nor to the nineteenth century—altho perhaps it has been carried further in our country and in our time than anywhere else. Modern Greek has recalled to its aid as much old Greek as it can assimilate. Sallust was accused by an acrid critic of having made a list of obsolete words, which he strove deliberately to reintroduce into Latin. This is, in effect, what Spenser sought to do with Chaucer's vocabulary; and it is curious to reflect that, owing, it may be, in part, to the example set by the author of the 'Faerie Queene,' the language of the 'Canterbury Tales' is far less strange, less remote, less archaic to us to-day than it was to the Elizabethans.

A rapid consumption of the vocabulary is going on constantly. Words are swiftly worn out and used up and thrown aside. New words are made or borrowed to fill the vacancies; and old words are impressed into service and forced to do double duty. No sooner is a new dictionary completed than the editor sets about his inevitable supplement. And the dictionary is not only of necessity incomplete: it is also inadequate in its definitions, for it may happen that a word will take on an added meaning while the big book is at the bindery. Our language is fluctuating always; and now one word and now another has expanded its content or has shrunk away into insignificance. No definition is surely stable for long. When Cotton Mather wrote in defense of his own style *disgust* was fairly equivalent to *dislike*; "and if a more massy way of writing be never so much disgusted at this day, a better gust will come on."

Once upon a time *to aggravate* meant to increase an offense; now it is often used as tho it meant to irritate. Formerly *calculated*—as in the sentence "it was *calculated* to do harm"—implied a deliberate intention to injure; now the idea of intention has been eliminated and the sentence is held to be roughly equivalent to "it was likely to do harm." *Verbal* is slowly getting itself accepted as synonymous with *oral*, in antithesis to *written*. *Lurid* was really *pale, wan, ghastly*; but how often of late has it been employed as tho it signified *red* or *ruddy* or *bloody*?

At first these new uses of these old words were slovenly and inadmissible inaccuracies, but by sheer insistence they are winning their pardon, until at last they will gain authority as they broaden down from precedent to precedent. It is well to be off with the old word before you are on with the new; and no writer who respects his mother-tongue is ever in haste to take up with words thus wrested from the primitive propriety.

But, as Dryden declared when justifying his modernizing of Chaucer's vocabulary, "Words are not like landmarks, so sacred as never to be removed; customs are changed, and even statutes are silently repealed when the reason ceases for which they were enacted." It was Dryden's "Cousin Swift" who once declared that "a nice man is a man of nasty ideas"—an assertion which I venture to believe to be wholly incomprehensible to-day to the young ladies of England in whose mouths *nice* means *agreeable* and *nasty* means *disagreeable*. *Nice* has suffered this inexplicable metamorphosis in the United States as well as in Great Britain, but *nasty* has not yet been emptied of its original offensiveness here as it has over there. And even in British speech the transformation is relatively recent; I think Stevenson was guilty of an anachronism in 'Weir of Hermiston' when he put it in the mouth of a young Scot.

If the Scotch have followed the evil example of the English in misusing *nasty*, the English in turn have twisted the *ilk* of North Britain to serve their own ends. *Of that ilk* is a phrase added to a man's surname to show that this name and the name of his estate are the same; thus Bradwardine of Bradwardine would be called "Bradwardine *of that ilk*." But it is not uncommon now to see a phrase like "people of that ilk," meaning obviously "people of that sort."

In like manner *awful* and *terrible* and *elegant* have been so misused as mere intensives that a careful writer now strikes them out when they come off the end of his pen in their original meaning. So *quite* no longer implies *completely* but is almost synonymous with *somewhat*—*quite poor* meaning *somewhat poor* and *quite good* meaning *pretty good*. *Unique* is getting to imply merely excellent or perhaps only unusual; its exact etymological value is departing forever. *Creole*, which should be applied only to Caucasian natives of tropical countries born of Latin parents, is beginning to carry with it in the vulgar tongue of to-day a vague suspicion of negro blood.

While the perversion of *nice* and *nasty* is British, there is an American perversion of *dirt* not unlike it. To most Americans, I think, *dirt* suggests *earth* or *soil* or *clay* or *dust*; to most Americans, I think, *dirt* no longer carries with it any suggestion of *dirtiness*. I have heard a mother send her little boy off to make mud-pies on condition that he used only "clean *dirt*"; and I know that a lawn-tennis ground of compacted earth is called a *dirt* court. Yet, tho the noun has thus been defecated, the adjective keeps its earlier force; and there even lingers something of the pristine value in the noun itself when it is employed in the picturesque idiom of the Rocky Mountains, where to be guilty of an underhand injury against any one is *to do him dirt*. Lovers of Western verse will recall how the frequenters of Casey's table d'hôte went to see "Modjesky as Cameel," and how they sat in silence until the break occurs between the lover and his mistress:

> At that Three-fingered Hoover says: "I'll chip into this game,
> And see if Red Hoss Mountain cannot reconstruct the same.
> I won't set by and see the feelin's of a lady hurt—
> Gol durn a critter, anyhow, that does a woman dirt!"

Here no doubt, we have crossed the confines of slang; but having done so, I venture upon an anecdote which will serve to show how completely sometimes the newer meaning of a word substitutes itself for the older. Two friends of mine were in a train of the elevated railroad, passing through that formerly craggy part of upper New York which was once called Shantytown and which now prefers to be known as Harlem. One of them drew the attention of the other to the capering young capricorns that sported over the blasted rocks by the side of the lofty track. "Just look at those kids," were the words he used. He was overheard by a boy of the streets sitting in the next seat, who glanced out of the window at once, but failed to discover the children he expected to behold. Whereupon he promptly looked up and corrected my friend. "Them's not kids," declared the urchin of Manhattan; "them's little goats!" In the mind of this native youngster there was no doubt at all as to the meaning of the word *kid*; to him it meant *child*; and he would have scorned any explanation that it ever had meant *young goat*.

In ignorance is certainty, and with increase of wisdom comes hesitancy. For example, what does the word *romantic* really mean? Few adjectives are harder worked in the history of modern literature; and no two of those who use it would agree upon its exact context. It suggests one set of circumstances to the student of English literature, a second set to a student of German literature, and a third to a student of French literature; while every student of comparative literature must echo Professor Kuno Francke's longing for "the formation of an international league for the suppression of the terms both *romanticism* and *classicism*."

Other words there are almost as ambiguous—*philology*, for example, and *college* and *chapel*. By *classical philology* we understand the study of all that survives of the civilizations of Greece and Rome, their languages, their literature, their laws, their arts. But has *Romance philology* or *Germanic philology* so broad a basis? Has *English philology*? To nine out of ten of us, this use of the word now seems to put stress on the study of linguistics as against the study of literature; to ninety-nine out of a hundred, I think, *philologist* suggests the narrow student of linguistics; and therefore the wider meaning seems likely soon to fall into innocuous desuetude.

The change in the application of *college* is still in process of accomplishment. In England a college was a place of instruction, sometimes independent (as Eton College, in which case it is really a high school) and sometimes a component part of a university (in which case the rest of the organization is not infrequently non-existent). An English university is not unlike a federation of colleges; and the relation of Merton and Magdalen to Oxford is not unlike that of Massachusetts and Virginia to the United States. In America *college* and *university* were long carelessly confused, as tho they were interconvertible terms; but of late a sharp distinction is being set up—a distinction quite different from that obtaining in England. In this new American usage, a *college* is a place where undergraduates are trained, and a *university* is a place where graduate-students are guided in research. Thus the college gives breadth, and the university adds depth. Thus the college provides general culture and the university provides the opportunity of specialization. If we accept this distinction,—and it has been accepted by all those who discuss the higher education in America,—we are forced to admit that the most of the self-styled universities of this country should be called colleges; and we are allowed to observe that the college and the university can exist side by side in the same institution, as at Harvard and at Columbia. We are forced also to admit that what is known in Great Britain as "University Extension" cannot fairly retain that title here in the United States, since its object is not the extension of university work, as we now understand the word *university* here; it is at most the extension of college work.

While this modification of the meaning of *college* is being made in America, a modification of *chapel* has been made in England. At first *chapel* described a subordinate part of a *church*, devoted to special services. By natural extension it came to denote a smaller edifice subsidiary to a large church, as Grace Church, in New York, was once a chapel of Trinity Church. But in the nineteenth century *chapel* came to be applied in England especially to the humbler meeting-houses of the various sects of dissenters, while *church* is reserved for the places of worship of the established religion. Thus Sir Walter Besant classifies the population of a riverside parish in London into those who go to *church* and those who go to *chapel*, having no doubt that all his British readers will understand the former to be Episcopalians and the latter Methodists or the like.

This is a Briticism not likely ever to be adopted in America. But another Briticism bids fair to have a better fortune. Living as they do on a little group of islands, the British naturally are in the habit of referring to the rest of Europe as the *Continent*. They run across the Channel to take a little tour "on the Continent." They speak of the pronunciation of Latin that obtains everywhere but in Great Britain and Ireland as the *continental* pronunciation. When they wish to differentiate their authors, for instance, from the French and the German and the Italians, they lump these last together as the *continental* authors. The division of Europe into *continental* and *British* is so convenient that it is certain to be adopted on this side of the Atlantic. Already has a New York literary review, after having had a series of papers on "Living Critics" (in which were included both British writers and American), followed it with a series of "Living Continental Critics" (in which the chief critics of France, Germany, Spain, and Scandinavia were considered). Yet there is no logic in this use of the word over here, since we Americans are not insular; and since North America is a continent just as Europe is. As it happens, the word *continental* in a wholly contradictory meaning is glorious in the history of the United States. Who does not know how,

> In their ragged regimentals,
> Stood the old Continentals,
>   Yielding not?

None the less will the convenience of this British use of the word outweigh its lack of logic in America—as convenience has so often overridden far more serious considerations. Language is only a tool, after all; and it must ever be shaped to fit the hand that uses it. This is why another illogical misuse of a word will get itself recognized as legitimate sooner or later—the limitations of *American* to mean only that which belongs to the United States. When we speak of American ideas we intend to exclude not only the ideas of South America but also those of Mexico and of Canada; we are really arrogating to ourselves a supremacy so overwhelming as to warrant our ignoring altogether all the other peoples having a right to share in the adjective. Our reason for this is that there is no national adjective available for us. We can speak of *Mexican* ideas and of *Canadian* ideas; but we cannot—or at least we do not and we will not—speak of *United Statesian* ideas. And this appropriation to ourselves of an adjective really the property of all the inhabitants of the continent seems to be perfectly acceptable to the only other group of those inhabitants speaking our language,—the English colonists to the north of us. On both sides of the Niagara River the smaller brother of the gigantic Horseshoe cataract is known as the "American fall." Even in the last century the British employed *American* to indicate the inhabitants of the thirteen colonies; and Dr. Johnson wrote in 1775: "That the *Americans* are able to bear taxation is indubitable." But our ownership of *American* as a national adjective, if tolerated by the Canadians and the British, is not admitted by those who do not speak our language. Probably to both the Italians and the Spaniards South America rather than North is the part of the world that rises in the mental vision when the word *American* is suddenly pronounced.

Another distinction not unlike this, but logical as well as convenient, is getting itself recognized. This distinction results from accepting the obvious fact that the literature of the English language has nowadays two independent divisions—that produced in the British Isles and that produced in the United States. The writers of both nations speak the English language, and therefore their works—whensoever these rise to the level of literature—belong to English literature. We are wont to call one division *American* literature, and we are beginning to see that logic will soon force us to call the other division *British* literature. Mr. Stedman has dealt with the poetry of the English language of the past sixty years in two volumes, one on the 'Victorian Poets,' and the other on the 'Poets of America,' and this serves to show how sharp is the line of separation. With his customary carefulness of epithet, Mr. Stedman in the preface to the earlier volume always uses *British* as the antithesis of *American*, reserving *English* as the broader adjective to cover both branches of our literature. Probably the many collections of the 'British Poets,' the 'British Novelists,' the 'British Theater,' were so called to allow the inclusion of works produced in the sister kingdoms; it is well to remember that Scott and Moore were neither of them Englishmen. There is a certain piquancy in the fact that the adjective *British*, available in the beginning of the nineteenth century because it included the Scotch and the Irish, is even more useful at the end of the nineteenth century because it differentiates the English, Scotch, and Irish, taken all together, from the Americans.

Telegram was denounced as a mismade word, and *cablegram* was rejected with abhorrence by all defenders of purity. Yet the firm establishment of *telegraph* and *telephone* made certain the ultimate acceptance of *telegram*. But *cablegram* is still on probation, and may fail of admission in the end, perhaps, because a part of the word seems to be better fitted for its purpose than the whole. A message received by the telegraph under the ocean is often curtly called a *cable*, as when a man says, "I've just had a cable from my wife in Paris." This, I think, is rather American than British; but it is akin to the British use of *wire* as synonymous with both *telegram* and *to telegraph*. An Englishman invites you to a house-party, and writes that he will meet you at the station "on a *wire*," intending to convey to you his desire that you should telegraph him the hour of your arrival. In a short story by Mr. Henry James, that most conscientious of recorders of British speech, he tells us that after *wires* and *counterwires* one of the characters of his tale was at last able to arrive at the house where the action takes place. The locution is hot from the verbal foundry; and it seems to imply what an American writer would have expressed by saying that there had been "telegraphing to and fro."

American, probably, is the verb *to process*, and also its past participle *processed*. When new methods of photo-engraving were introduced here in the United States, a black-and-white artist would express a preference either to have his drawing engraved on wood or have it reproduced mechanically by a photo-engraving process; and as he needed a brief word to describe this latter act, one was promptly forthcoming, and he asked, "Is this thing of mine to be engraved or *processed*?" The word *half-tone* seems also to be of American manufacture; and it describes one of these methods of photo-engraving. It is not only a noun, but also, on occasions, a verb; and the artist will ask if his wash-drawing is to be *half-toned*. Of necessity the several improvements in the art of photo-engraving brought with them a variety of new terms absolutely essential in the terminology of the craft, most of them remaining hidden in the technical vocabulary, altho now and again one or another has thrust itself up into the general language.

Any attempt to declare the British or the American origin of an idiom is most precarious; and he who ventures upon it has need of double caution. When a friend of mine asked the boy at the door of the club if it was still raining, and was answered, "No, sir; it's *fairing up* now," he was at first inclined to think that he had captured an Americanism hitherto unknown and delightfully fresh; but he consulted the Century Dictionary, only to find that it was a Scoticism,—there was even a quotation from Stevenson's 'Inland Voyage,'—and that it was not uncommon in the southwestern states. And when Captain Mahan brought out the difference between *preparation* for war and *preparedness* for war, this friend was ready to credit the naval historian with the devising not only of a most valuable distinction but also of a most useful word; but a dip into the Century Dictionary again revealed that a Scotchman had not waited for an American to use the word, and that it had been employed by Bain, not even as tho it was a novelty.

Once in the pages of Hawthorne, who was affluent in words and artistically adroit in his management of them, I met a phrase that pleased me mightily, "a *heterogeny* of things"; and I find *heterogeny* duly collected in the Century Dictionary but without any quotation from Hawthorne. Another word of Hawthorne's in the 'Blithedale Romance' is *improvability*: "In my own behalf, I rejoice that I could once think better of the world's *improvability* than it deserved." This I fancy may be Hawthorne's very own; but it is in the Century Dictionary, all the same, and without any indication of its origin. Quite possibly the New England romancer disinterred it from some forgotten tome of the "somniferous school of literature," as he had humorously entitled the writings of his theological ancestors.

There is a word of Abraham Lincoln's that I long for the right to use. Mr. Noah Brooks has recorded that he once heard the President speak of a certain man as *interruptious*. This adjective conveys a delicate shade of meaning not discoverable in any other; it may not be inscribed in the bead-roll of the King's English, but it was a specimen of the President's English; and has any Speech from the Throne in this century really rivaled the force and felicity of the Second Inaugural?

It was not the liberator of the negro but one of the freedmen themselves who made offhand use of a delicious word, for which it is probably hopeless for us to expect acceptance, however useful the new term might prove. During a debate in the legislature of South Carolina in the Reconstruction days, a sable ally of the carpet-baggers rose to repel the taunts of his opponents, declaring energetically that he hurled back with scorn all their *insinuendos*. The word holds a middle ground between *insinuation* and *innuendo*; and between the two it has scant chance of survival. But it is an amusing attempt, for all its failure; and it would have given pleasure to the author of 'Alice in Wonderland.' And how many of Lewis Carroll's own verbal innovations, wantonly manufactured for his sport, are likely to get themselves admitted into the language of literature? *Chortle* stands the best chance of them all, I think; and I believe that many a man has said that he *chortled*, with no thought of the British bard who ingeniously devised the quaint vocable.

So Mr. W. S. Gilbert's *burgle* seems to be winning its way into general use. At first those who employed it followed the example of the comic lyrist, and did so with humorous intent; but of late it is beginning to serve those who are wholly devoid of humor. Perhaps the verb *to burgle* (from the noun *burglar*) supplied the analogy on which was made the verb *to ush* (from the noun *usher*). With my own ears I once heard a well-known clergyman in New York express the thanks of the congregation to "the gentlemen who *ush* for us."

It is well that strange uses like these do not win early acceptance into our speech—that there should be alert challengers at the portal to cry "Halt!" and to examine a newcomer's credentials. It is well also that the stranger should have leave to prove his usefulness and so in time gain admittance even to the inner sanctuary of the language. John Dryden discussed the reception into English of new words and phrases with the sturdy common sense which was one of the characteristics most endearing him to us as a true type of the man of letters who was also a man of the world. "It is obvious," he wrote in his 'Defense of the Epilog,' "that we have admitted many, some of which we wanted, and therefore our language is the richer for them, as it would be by importation of bullion; others are rather ornamental than necessary; yet by their admission the language is become more courtly and our thoughts are better dressed."

Historians of the language have had no difficulty in bringing together a mass of quotations from the British writers of the eighteenth century to show that they were then possessed of the belief that it was feasible and necessary to set bounds to the growth of English. They were afraid that the changes going on in the language would make it "impossible for succeeding ages to read or appreciate the literature produced." In his interesting and instructive lecture on the 'Evolution of English Lexicography,' Dr. Murray remarks that "to us of a later age, with our fuller knowledge of the history of language, and our wider experience of its fortunes, when it has to be applied to entirely new fields of knowledge, such as have been opened to us since the birth of modern science, this notion seems childlike and pathetic. But it was eminently characteristic of the eighteenth century."

It is small wonder therefore that this absurd notion infected two of the most characteristic figures of the eighteenth century—Johnson and Franklin. Dr. Johnson set forth in the plan of his dictionary that "one great end of this undertaking is to fix the English language." Even so shrewd a student of all things as was Franklin seems to have accepted this current fallacy. When he acknowledged the dedication of Noah Webster's 'Dissertations on the English Language,' he declared that he could not "but applaud your zeal for preserving the purity of our language, both in its expressions and pronunciation." Then, as tho to prove to us, once for all, the futility of all efforts to "fix the language" and to "preserve its purity," Franklin picks out half a dozen novelties of phrase and begs that Webster will use his "authority in reprobating them." Among these innovations that Franklin disapproved of are *improved, noticed, advocated, progressed*, and *opposed*.

This letter to Webster was written in 1789; and already in 1760 Franklin had yielded to certain of David Hume's criticisms upon his parts of speech: "I thank you for your friendly admonition relating to some unusual words in the pamphlet. It will be of service to me. The *pejorate* and the *colonize*, since they are not in common use here, I give up as bad; for certainly in writings intended for persuasion and for general information, one cannot be too clear; and every expression in the least obscure is a fault. The *unshakable*, too, tho clear, I give up as rather low. The introducing new words, where we are already possessed of old ones sufficiently expressive, I confess must be generally wrong, as it tends to change the language."

With all his intellect and all his insight and all his common sense—and with this most precious quality Franklin was better furnished than either Johnson or Dryden—he could not foresee that *to notice* and *to advocate* and *to colonize* were words without which the English language could not do its work in the world. And when he gives up *unshakable* "as rather low" he stands confessed as a contemporary of the men whom Fielding and Goldsmith girded at. In spite of the example of Steele and Addison, in spite of his own vigorous directness in 'Poor Richard' and in all his political pamphlets, Franklin feels that there is and that there ought to be a wide gap between the English that is spoken and the English that is written. He did not perceive that spoken English, with all its hazardous expressions, its clipped words, its violent metaphors, its picturesque slang, its slovenly clumsiness, is none the less the proving-ground of the literary vocabulary, which is forever tending to self-exhaustion.

Nobody has better stated the wiser attitude of a writer toward the tools of his trade than Professor Harry Thurston Peck in his incisive discussion of 'What is Good English?' He begins by noting that "the English language, as a whole, is the richest of all modern tongues, and it is not to be bounded by the comparatively narrow limits of its literature. There exists, as well, the easy, fluent usage of conversation, and there is also the strong, simple, homely speech of the common people, rooted in plain Saxon, smacking of the soil, and having a sturdy power about it that is unsurpassable for downright force and blunt directness." And Professor Peck, having pointed out how an artist in words is free to avail himself of the term he needs from books or from life, declares that "the writer of the best English is he whose language responds exactly to his mood and thought, now thundering and surging with the majestic words whose immediate ancestry is Roman, now rippling and singing with the smooth harmonies of later speech, now forging ahead with the irresistible energy of the Saxon, and now laughing and wantoning in the easy lightness of our modern phrase."

VII
THE NATURALIZATION OF FOREIGN WORDS

When Taine was praising that earliest of analytical novels, the 'Princess of Cleves,' he noted the simplicity of Madame de Lafayette's style. "Half of the words we use are unknown to Madame de Lafayette," he declared. "She is like the painters of old, who could make every shade with only five or six colors." And he asserts that "there is no easier reading" than this story of Madame de Lafayette's; "a child could understand without effort all her expressions and all her phrases.... Nowadays every writer is a pedant, and every style is obscure. All of us have read three or four centuries, and three or four literatures. Philosophy, science, art, criticism have weighted us with their discoveries and their jargons."

This is true enough, no doubt; and one of the strange phenomenons of the nineteenth century was the sudden and enormous swelling of our vocabularies. Perhaps the distention of the dictionary is even more obvious in English than in French, for there are now three times as many human beings using the language of Shakspere as there are now using the language of Molière; and while the speakers of French are compacted in one country and take their tone from its capital, the speakers of English are scattered in the four quarters of the earth, and they use each man his own speech in his own fashion. From the wider variety of interests among those who speak English, our language is perforce more hospitable to foreign words than French needs to be, since it is used rather by a conservative people who prefer to stay at home.

Perhaps the French are at times even too inhospitable to the foreign phrase. A friend of mine who came to the reading of M. Paul Bourget's 'Essais de Psychologie Contemporaine,' fresh from the perusal of the German philosophers, told me that he was pained by M. Bourget's vain effort to express the thoughts the French author had absorbed from the Germans. It seemed as tho M. Bourget were struggling for speech, and could not say what was in his mind for lack of words in his native tongue capable of conveying his meaning. Of course it must be remembered that German philosophy is vague and fluctuating, and that the central thought is often obscured by a penumbra, while French is the most precise of languages. Those who are proud of it have declared that what is not clear is not French. When Hegel was asked by a traveler from Paris for a succinct statement of his system of philosophy, he smiled and answered that it could not be explained summarily—"especially in French!"

The English language extends a warmer welcome to the foreign term, and also exercises more freely its right to make a word for itself whenever one is needed. The manufactured article is not always satisfactory, but if it gets into general use, no further evidence is required that it was made to supply a genuine want. *Scientist*, for example, is an ugly word (altho an invention of Whewell's), and yet it was needed. How necessary it was can be seen by any reader of the late F. W. H. Myers's essay on 'Science and a Future Life,' who notes that Myers refused resolutely to use it, altho it conveys exactly the meaning the author wanted, and that the British writer preferred to employ instead the French *savant*, which does not—etymologically at least—contain his full intention. Myers's fastidiousness did not, however, prevent his using *creationist* as an adjective, and also *bonism* as a substitute for *optimism*, "with no greater barbarism in the form of the word and more accuracy in the meaning."

Just as Myers used *savant* so Ruskin was willing to arrest the rhythm of a fine passage by the obtrusion of two French words: "A well-educated gentleman may not know many languages; may not be able to speak any but his own; may have read very few books. But whatever language he knows, he knows precisely; whatever word he pronounces, he pronounces rightly; above all, he is learned in the peerage of words; knows the words of true descent and ancient blood at a glance from words of modern *canaille*; remembers all their ancestry, their intermarriages, distantest relationships, and the extent to which they were admitted, and offices they hold among the national *noblesse* of words, at any time and in any country." There seems to be little or no excuse for the employment here of *noblesse*=nobility; and as for *canaille*, perhaps Ruskin held that to be a French word on the way to become an English word—a naturalization not likely to take place without a marked modification of the original pronunciation, which is difficult for the English mouth.

Every one who loves good English cannot but have a healthy hatred for the style of a writer who insists on bespattering his pages with alien words and foreign phrases; and yet we are more tolerant, I think, toward a term taken from one of the dead languages than toward one derived from any of the living tongues. Probably the bishop who liked now and then to cite a Hebrew sentence was oversanguine in his explanation that "everybody knows a little Hebrew." It is said that even a Latin quotation is now no longer certain to be recognized in the British House of Commons; and yet it was a British statesman who declared that, altho there was no necessity for a gentleman to know Latin, he ought at least to have forgotten it.

For a bishop to quote Hebrew is now pedantic, no doubt, and even for the inferior clergy to quote Latin. It is pedantic, but it is not indecorous; whereas a French quotation in the pulpit, or even the use of a single French word, like *savant*, for example, would seem to most of us almost a breach of the proprieties. It would strike us, perhaps, not merely as a social solecism, but somehow as morally reprehensible. A preacher who habitually cited French phrases would be in danger of the council. To picture Jonathan Edwards as using the language of Voltaire is impossible. That a French quotation should seem more incongruous in the course of a religious argument than a Latin, a Greek, or a Hebrew quotation, is perhaps to be ascribed to the fact that many of us hold the Parisians to be a more frivolous people than the Romans, the Athenians, or the Israelites; and as the essay of Mr. Myers was a religious argument, this may be one reason why his employment of *savant* was unfortunate.

Another reason is suggested by Professor Dowden's shrewd remark that "a word, like a comet, has a tail as well as a head." An adroit craftsman in letters is careful always that the connotations of the terms he chooses shall be in accord with the tone of his thesis. It may be disputed whether *savant* denotes the same thing as *scientist*, but it can hardly be denied that the connotations of the two words are wholly different. For my own part, some lingering memory of Abbott's 'Napoleon,' absorbed in boyhood, links the wise men of France with the donkeys of Egypt, because whenever the Mameluke cavalry threatened the French squares the cry went up, "Asses and *savants* to the center!"

After all, it is perhaps rather a question whether or not *savant* is now an English noun. There are many French words knocking at the door of the

English language and asking for admission. Is *littoral* for *shore* now an English noun? Is *blond* an English adjective meaning *light-haired* and opposed to *brunette*? Is *brunette* itself really Anglicized? (I ask this in spite of the fact that a friend of mine once read in a country newspaper a description of a *brunette* horse.) Has *inedited* for *unpublished* won its way into our language finally? Lowell gave it his warrant, at least by using it in his 'Letters'; but I confess that it has always struck me as liable to confusion with *unedited*.

Foreign words must always be allowed to land on our coasts without a passport; yet if any of them linger long enough to warrant a belief that they may take out their papers sooner or later, we must decide at last whether or not they are likely to be desirable residents of our dictionary; and if we determine to naturalize them, we may fairly enough insist on their renouncing their foreign allegiance. They must cast in their lot with us absolutely, and be bound by our laws only. The French *chaperon*, for example, has asked for admission to our vocabulary, and the application has been granted, so that we have now no hesitation in recording that Daisy Miller was *chaperoned* by Becky Sharp at the last ball given by the Marquis of Steyne; and we have even changed the spelling of the noun to correspond better with our Anglicized pronunciation, thus *chaperone*. Thus *technique* has changed its name to *technic*, and is made welcome; so early as 1867 Matthew Arnold used *technic* in his 'Study of Celtic Literature,' but even now his fellow-islanders are slow in following his example. Thus *employé* is accepted in the properly Anglicized form of *employee*. Thus the useful *clôture* undergoes a sea-change and becomes the English *closure*. And why not *cotery* also? I note that in his 'Studies in Literature,' published in 1877, Professor Dowden put *technique* into italics as tho it was still a foreign word, while he left *coterie* in ordinary type as tho it had been adopted into English.

So *toilette* has been abbreviated to *toilet*; at least, I should have said so without any hesitation if I had not recently seen the foreign spelling reappearing repeatedly in the pages of Robert Louis Stevenson's 'Amateur Emigrant'—and this in the complete Edinburgh edition prepared by Mr. Sidney Colvin. To find a Gallic spelling in the British prose of Stevenson is a surprise, especially since the author of the 'Dynamiter' is on record as a contemner of another orthographic Gallicism. In a foot-note to 'More New

Arabian Nights' Stevenson declares that "any writard who writes *dynamitard* shall find in me a never-resting fightard."

I should like to think that the naturalized *literator* was supplanting the alien *littérateur,* but I cannot claim confidence as to the result. *Literator* is a good English word: I have found it in the careful pages of Lockhart's 'Life of Scott'; and I make no doubt that it can prove a much older pedigree than that. It seems to me a better word by far than *literarian,* which the late Fitzedward Hall manufactured for his own use "some time in the fifties," and which he defended against a British critic who denounced it as "atrocious." Hall, praising the word of his own making, declared that "to *literatus* or *literator,* for *literary person* or a longer phrase of equivalent import, there are obvious objections." Nobody, to the best of my belief, ever attempted to use in English the Latin *literatus,* altho its plural Poe made us familiar with by his series of papers on the 'Literati of America.' Since Poe's death the word has ceased to be current, altho it was not uncommon in his day.

Perhaps one of the obvious objections to *literatus* is that if it be treated as an English word the plural it forms is not pleasant to the ear—*literatuses*. Here, indeed, is a moot point: How does a foreign word make its plural in English? Some years ago Mr. C. F. Thwing, writing in *Harper's Bazar* on the college education of young women, spoke of *foci*. Mr. Churton Collins, preparing a book about the study of English literature in the British universities, expressed his desire "to raise Greek, now gradually falling out of our *curricula* and degenerating into the cachet and shibboleth of cliques of pedants, to its proper place in education." Here we see Mr. Thwing and Mr. Collins treating *focus* and *curriculum* as words not yet assimilated by our language, and therefore required to assume the Latin plural.

Does not this suggest a certain lack of taste on the part of these writers? If *focus* and *curriculum* are not good English words, what need is there to employ them when you are using the English language to convey your thoughts? There are occasions, of course, where the employment of a foreign term is justifiable, but they must always be very rare. The imported word which we really require we had best take to ourselves, incorporating it in the language, treating it thereafter absolutely as an English word, and giving it the regular English plural. If the word we use is so foreign that we should print it in italics, then of course the plural should be formed according to the rules of the foreign language from which it has been borrowed; but if it has become so acclimated in our tongue that we should not think of underlining it, then surely it is English enough to take an English plural. If *cherub* is now English, its plural is the English *cherubs*, and not the Hebrew *cherubim*. If *criterion* is now English, its plural is the English *criterions*, and not the Greek *criteria*. If *formula* is now English, its plural is the English *formulas*, and not the Latin *formulæ*. If *bureau* is now English, its plural is the English *bureaus*, and not the French *bureaux*.

What is the proper plural in English of *cactus*? of *vortex*? of *antithesis*? of *phenomenon*? In a volume on the 'Augustan Age,' in Professor George Saintsbury's 'Periods of European Literature,' we find *lexica*—a masterpiece of petty pedantry and of pedantic pettiness. As Landor made himself say in his dialog with Archdeacon Hare, "There is an affectation of scholarship in compilers of spelling-books, and in the authors they follow for examples, when they bring forward *phenomena* and the like. They might as well bring forward *mysteria*. We have no right to tear Greek and Latin declensions out of their grammars: we need no *vortices* when we have *vortexes* before us; and while we have *memorandums*, *factotums*, and *ultimatums*, let our shepherd dogs bring back to us by the ear such as have wandered from the flock."

Landor's own scholarship was too keen and his taste was too fine for him not to abhor such affectation. He held that Greek and Latin words had no business in an English sentence unless they had been frankly acclimated in the English language, and that one of the conditions of this acclimatizing was the shedding of their original plurals. And that this is also the common-sense view of most users of English is obvious enough. Nobody now ventures to write *factota* or *ultimata*; and even *memoranda* seems to be vanishing. But *phenomena* and *data* still survive; and so do *errata* and *candelabra*. Whatever may be the fate of *phenomena*, that of the three other words may perhaps be like unto the fate of *opera*—which is also a Latin plural and which has become an English singular. We speak unhesitatingly of the *operas* of Rossini; are we going, in time, to speak unhesitatingly of the *candelabras* of Cellini? In his vigorous article on the orthography of the French language—which is still almost as chaotic and illogical as the orthography of the English language—Sainte-Beuve noted as a singular peculiarity the fact that *errata* had got itself recognized as a French singular, but that it did not yet take the French plural; thus we see *un errata* and *des errata.*

It is true also that when we take over a term from another language we ought to be sure that it really exists in the other language. For lack of observance of this caution we find ourselves now in possession of phrases like *nom de plume* and *déshabille,* of which the French never heard. And even when we have assured ourselves of the existence of the word in the foreign language, it behooves us then to assure ourselves also of its exact meaning before we take it for our own. In his interesting and instructive book about 'English Prose,' Professor Earle reminds us that the French of Stratford-atte-Bowe is not yet an extinct species; and he adds in a note that "the word *levée* seems to be another genuine instance of the same insular dialect," since it is not French of any date, but an English improvement upon the verb (or substantive) *lever,* "getting up in the morning."

An example even more extraordinary than any of these, I think, will occur to those of us who are in the habit of glancing through the theatrical announcements of the American newspapers. This is the taking of the French word *vaudeville* to designate what was once known as a "variety show" and what is now more often called a "specialty entertainment." For any such interpretation of *vaudeville* there is no warrant whatever in French. Originally the "vaudeville" was a satiric ballad, bristling with hits at the times, and therefore closely akin to the "topical song" of to-day; and it is at this stage of its evolution that Boileau asserted that

Le Français, né malin, créa le vaudeville.

In time there came to be spoken words accompanying those sung, and thus the "vaudeville" expanded slowly into a little comic play in which there were one or more songs. Of late the Parisian "vaudeville" has been not unlike the London "musical farce." At no stage of its career had the "vaudeville" anything to do with the "variety show"; and yet to the average American to-day the two words seem synonymous. There was even organized in New York, in the fall of 1892, a series of subscription suppers during which "specialty entertainments" were to be given; and in spite of the fact that the organizers were presumably persons who had traveled, they called their society the "Vaudeville Club," altho no real "vaudeville" was ever presented before the members during its brief and inglorious career. Of course explanation and protest are now equally futile. The meaning of the word is forever warped beyond correction; and for the future here in America a "vaudeville performance" is a "variety show," no matter what it may be or may have been in France. When the people as a whole accept a word as having a certain meaning, that is and must be the meaning of the word thereafter; and there is no use in kicking against the pricks.

The fate in English of another French term is even now trembling in the balance. This is the word *née*. The French have found a way out of the difficulty of indicating easily the maiden name of a married woman; they write unhesitatingly about Madame Machin, *née* Chose; and the Germans have a like idiom. But instead of taking a hint from the French and the Germans, and thus of speaking about Mrs. Brown, *born* Gray, as they do, not a few English writers have simply borrowed the actual French word, and so we read about Mrs. Black, *née* White. As usual, this borrowing is dangerous; and the temptation seems to be irresistible to destroy the exact meaning of *née* by using it in the sense of "formerly." Thus in the 'Letters of Matthew Arnold, 1848-88,' collected and arranged by Mr. George W. E. Russell, the editor supplies in foot-notes information about the persons whose names appear in the correspondence. In one of these annotations we read that the wife of Sir Anthony de Rothschild was "*née* Louisa Montefiore" (i. 165), and in another that the Hon. Mrs. Eliot Yorke was "*née* Annie de Rothschild" (ii. 160). Now, neither of these ladies was *born* with a given name as well as a family name. It is obvious that the editor has chosen arbitrarily to wrench the meaning of *née* to suit his own convenience, a proceeding of which I venture to think that Matthew Arnold himself would certainly have disapproved. In fact, I doubt if Mr. Russell is not here guilty of an absurdity almost as obvious as that charged against a wealthy western lady now residing at the capital of the United States, who is said to have written her name on the register of a New York hotel thus: "Mrs. Blank, Washington, *née* Chicago."

Why is it that the wandering stars of the theatrical firmament are wont to display themselves in a *répertoire* when it would be so much easier for them to make use of a *repertory*? And why does the teacher of young and ambitious singers insist on calling his school a *conservatoire* when it would assert its rank just as well if it was known as a *conservatory*? What strange freak of chance has led so many of the women who have made themselves masters of the technic of the piano to announce themselves as *pianistes* in the vain belief that *pianiste* is the feminine of *pianist*? How comes it that a man capable of composing so scholarly a book as the 'Greek Drama' of Mr. Lionel D. Barnett really is should be guilty of saying that certain declamations in the later theater "were adapted to the style of popular *artistes*"? And why does Mr. Andrew Lang (in his 'Angling Sketches') write about the *asphalte*, when the obvious English is either *asphalt* or *asphaltum*?

And yet Mr. Lang, himself convicted of this dereliction, has no hesitation in objecting to a "delightful grammatical form which closes a scene in one of the new rag-bag journals. The author gets his characters off the stage with the announcement: 'They exit.' He seems to think that *exit* is a verb. I *exit*, he *exits*, they *exit*. It would be interesting to learn how he translates *exeunt omnes*. One is accustomed to 'a *penetralia*' from young lions, and to 'a *strata*,' but 'they *exit*' is original."

But the verb *to exit* is not original with the writer in the new rag-bag journal. It has been current in England for three quarters of a century at least, and it can be found in the pages of that vigorously written pair of volumes, Mrs. Trollope's 'Domestic Manners of the Americans' (published in 1831), in the picturesque passage in which she describes how the American women, left alone, "all console themselves together for whatever they may have suffered in keeping awake by taking more tea, coffee, hot cake and custard, hoe-cake, johnny-cake, waffle-cake and dodger-cake, pickled peaches and preserved cucumbers, ham, turkey, hung-beef, apple-sauce, and pickled oysters, than ever were prepared in any other country of the known world. After this massive meal is over, they return to the drawing-room, and it always appeared to me that they remained together as long as they could bear it, and then they rise *en masse*, cloak, bonnet, shawl, and exit."

The verb *to exit*, with the full conjugation Mr. Lang thought so strange, has long been common among theatrical folk. The stage-manager will tell the leading lady "You *exit* here, and she *exits* up left." The theatrical folk, who probably first brought the verb into use, did not borrow it from the Latin, as Mr. Lang seems to suppose; they simply made a verb of the existing English noun *exit*, meaning a way out. We old New-Yorkers who can recall the time when Barnum's Museum stood at the corner of Broadway and Ann Street, remember also the signs which used to declare

> THIS WAY
> TO THE
> GRAND EXIT

and we have not forgotten the facile anecdote of the countryman who went wonderingly to discover what manner of strange beast the "exit" might be, and who unexpectedly found himself in the street outside.

The unfortunate remark of Mr. Lang was due to his happening not to recall the fact that *exit* had become, first, an English noun, and, second, an English verb. When once it was Anglicized, it had all the rights of a native; it was a citizen of no mean country. The principle which it is well to keep in mind in any consideration of the position in English of terms once foreign is that no word can serve two masters. The English language is ever ravenous and voracious; its appetite is insatiable. It is forever taking over words from strange tongues, dead and alive. These words are but borrowed at first, and must needs conform to all the grammatical peculiarities of their native speech. But some of them are sooner or later firmly incorporated into English; and thereafter they must cease to obey any laws but those of the language into which they have been adopted. Either a word is English or it is not; and a decision on this point is rarely difficult.

(1895-1900)

VIII
THE FUNCTION OF SLANG

It is characteristic of the interest which science is now taking in things formerly deemed unworthy of consideration that philologists no longer speak of slang in contemptuous terms. Perhaps, indeed, it was not the scholar, but the amateur philologist, the mere literary man, who affected to despise slang. To the trained investigator into the mutations of language and into the transformations of the vocabulary, no word is too humble for respectful consideration; and it is from the lowly, often, that the most valuable lessons are learned. But until recently few men of letters ever mentioned slang except in disparagement and with a wish for its prompt extirpation. Even professed students of speech, like Trench and Alford (now sadly shorn of their former authority), are abundant in declarations of abhorrent hostility. De Quincey, priding himself on his independence and on his iconoclasm, was almost alone in saying a good word for slang.

There is this excuse for the earlier author who treated slang with contumely, that the differentiation of *slang* from *cant* was not complete in his day. *Cant* is the dialect of a class, often used correctly enough, as far as grammar is concerned, but often also unintelligible to those who do not belong to the class or who are not acquainted with its usages. *Slang* was at first the *cant* of thieves, and this seems to have been its only meaning until well into the present century. In 'Redgauntlet,' for example, published in 1824, Scott speaks of the "thieves' Latin called *slang*." Sometime during the middle of the century *slang* seems to have lost this narrow limitation, and to have come to signify a word or a phrase used with a meaning not recognized in polite letters, either because it had just been invented, or because it had passed out of memory. While *cant*, therefore, was a language within a language, so to speak, and not to be understanded of the people, *slang* was a collection of colloquialisms gathered from all sources, and all bearing alike the bend sinister of illegitimacy.

Certain of its words were unquestionably of very vulgar origin, being survivals of the "thieves' Latin" Scott wrote about. Among these are *pal* and *cove,* words not yet admitted to the best society. Others were merely arbitrary misapplications of words of good repute, such as the employment of *awfully* and *jolly* as synonyms for *very*—as intensives, in short. Yet others were violent metaphors, like *in the soup, kicking the bucket, holding up* (a stage-coach). Others, again, were the temporary phrases which spring up, one scarcely knows how, and flourish unaccountably for a few months, and then disappear forever, leaving no sign; such as *shoo-fly* in America and *all serene* in England.

An analysis of modern slang reveals the fact that it is possible to divide the words and phrases of which it is composed into four broad classes, of quite different origin and of very varying value. Toward two of these classes it may be allowable to feel the contempt so often expressed for slang as a whole. Toward the other two classes such a feeling is wholly unjustifiable, for they are performing an inestimable service to the language.

Of the two unworthy classes, the first is that which includes the survivals of the "thieves' Latin," the vulgar terms used by vulgar men to describe vulgar things. This is the slang which the police-court reporter knows and is fond of using profusely. This is the slang which Dickens introduced to literature. This class of slang it is which is mainly responsible for the ill repute of the word. Much of the dislike for slang felt by people of delicate taste is, however, due to the second class, which includes the ephemeral phrases fortuitously popular for a season, and then finally forgotten once for all. These mere catchwords of the moment are rarely foul, as the words and phrases of the first class often are, but they are unfailingly foolish. *There you go with your eye out,* which was accepted as a humorous remark in London, and *Where did you get that hat?* which had a like fleeting vogue in New York, are phrases as inoffensive as they are flat. These temporary terms come and go, and are forgotten swiftly. Probably most readers of Forcythe Wilson's 'Old Sergeant' need now to have it explained to them that during the war a *grape-vine* meant a lying rumor.

It must be said, however, that even in the terms of the first class there is a striving upward, a tendency to disinfect themselves, as any reader of Grose's 'Dictionary of the Vulgar Tongue' must needs remark when he discovers that phrases used now with perfect freedom had a secret significance in the last century. There are also innuendos not a few in certain of Shakspere's best-known plays which fortunately escape the notice of all but the special student of the Elizabethan vocabulary.

The other two classes of slang stand on a different footing. Altho they suffer from the stigma attached to all slang by the two classes already characterized, they serve a purpose. Indeed, their utility is indisputable, and it was never greater than it is to-day. One of these classes consists of old and forgotten phrases or words, which, having long lain dormant, are now struggling again to the surface. The other consists of new words and phrases, often vigorous and expressive, but not yet set down in the literary lexicon, and still on probation. In these two classes we find a justification for the existence of slang—for it is the function of slang to be a feeder of the vocabulary. Words get threadbare and dried up; they come to be like evaporated fruit, juiceless and tasteless. Now it is the duty of slang to provide substitutes for the good words and true which are worn out by hard service. And many of the recruits slang has enlisted are worthy of enrolment among the regulars. When a blinded conservative is called a *mossback*, who is so dull as not to perceive the poetry of the word? When an actor tells us how the traveling company in which he was engaged got *stranded*, who does not recognize the force and the felicity of the expression? And when we hear a man declare that he would to-day be rich if only his foresight had been equal to his *hindsight*, who is not aware of the value of the phrase? No wonder is it that the verbal artist hankers after such words which renew the lexicon of youth! No wonder is it that the writer who wishes to present his thought freshly seeks these words with the bloom yet on them, and neglects the elder words desiccated as tho for preservation in a herbarium!

The student of slang is surprised that he is able to bring forward an honorable pedigree for many words so long since fallen from their high estate that they are now treated as upstarts when they dare to assert themselves. Words have their fates as well as men and books; and the ups and downs of a phrase are often almost as pathetic as those of a man. It has been said that the changes of fortune are so sudden here in these United States that it is only three generations from shirt sleeves to shirt sleeves. The English language is not quite so fast as the American people, but in the English language it is only three centuries from shirt sleeves to shirt sleeves. What could seem more modern, more western even, than *deck* for *pack* of cards, and *to lay out* or to *lay out cold* for *to knockdown*? Yet these are both good old expressions, in decay no longer, but now insisting on their right to a renewed life. *Deck* is Elizabethan, and we find in Shakspere's 'King Henry VI.' (part iii., act v., sc. i.) that

The king was slyly finger'd from the deck.

To lay out in its most modern sense is very early English.

Even more important than this third class of slang expressions is the fourth, containing the terms which are, so to speak, serving their apprenticeship, and as yet uncertain whether or not they will be admitted finally into the gild of good English. These terms are either useful or useless; they either satisfy a need or they do not; they therefore live or die according to the popular appreciation of their value. If they expire, they pass into the limbo of dead-and-gone slang, than which there is no blacker oblivion. If they survive it is because they have been received into the literary language, having appealed to the perceptions of some master of the art and craft of speech, under whose sponsorship they are admitted to full rights. Thus we see that slang is a training-school for new expressions, only the best scholars getting the diploma which confers longevity, the others going surely to their fate.

Sometimes these new expressions are words only, sometimes they are phrases. *To go back on*, for instance, and *to give one's self away* are specimens of the phrase characteristic of this fourth and most interesting class of slang at its best. In its creation of phrases like these, slang is what idiom was before language stiffened into literature, and so killed its earlier habit of idiom-making. After literature has arrived, and after the schoolmaster is abroad, and after the printing-press has been set up in every hamlet, the idiom-making faculty of a language is atrophied by disuse. Slang is sometimes, and to a certain extent, a survival of this faculty, or at least a substitute for its exercise. In other words (and here I take the liberty of quoting from a private letter of one of the foremost authorities on the history of English, Professor Lounsbury), "slang is an effort on the part of the users of language to say something more vividly, strongly, concisely than the language as existing permits it to be said"; and he adds that slang is therefore "the source from which the decaying energies of speech are constantly refreshed."

Being contrary to the recognized standards of speech, slang finds no mercy at the hands of those who think it their duty to uphold the strict letter of the law. Nothing amazes an investigator more, and nothing more amuses him, than to discover that thousands of words now secure in our speech were once denounced as interlopers. "There is death in the dictionary," said Lowell, in his memorable linguistic essay prefixed to the second series of the 'Biglow Papers'; "and where language is too strictly limited by convention, the ground for expression to grow in is limited also, and we get a *potted* literature—Chinese dwarfs instead of healthy trees." And in the paper on Dryden he declared that "a language grows and is not made." Pedants are ever building the language about with rules of iron in a vain effort to keep it from growing naturally and according to its needs.

It is true that *cab* and *mob* are clipped words, and there has always been a healthy dislike of any clipping of the verbal currency. But *consols* is firmly established. Two clipped words there are which have no friends—*gents* and *pants*. Dr. Holmes has put them in the pillory of a couplet:

> The things named *pants*, in certain documents,
> A word not made for gentlemen, but *gents*.

And recently a sign, suspended outside a big Broadway building, announced that there were "Hands wanted on pants," the building being a clothing factory, and not, as one might suppose, a boys' school.

The slang of a metropolis, be that where you will, in the United States or in Great Britain, in France or in Germany, is nearly always stupid. There is neither fancy nor fun in the Parisian's *Ohé Lambert* or *on dirait du veau*, nor in the Londoner's *all serene* or *there you go with your eye out*—catchwords which are humorous, if humorous they are, only by general consent and for some esoteric reason. It is to such stupid phrases of a fleeting popularity that Dr. Holmes refers, no doubt, when he declares that "the use of slang, or cheap generic terms, as a substitute for differentiated specific expressions is at once a sign and a cause of mental atrophy." And this use of slang is far more frequent in cities, where people often talk without having anything to say, than in the country, where speech flows slowly.

Perhaps the more highly civilized a population is, the more it has parted with the power of pictorial phrase-making. It may be that a certain lawlessness of life is the cause of a lawlessness of language. Of all metropolitan slang that of the outlaws is most vigorous. It was after Vidocq had introduced thieves' slang into polite society that Balzac, always a keen observer and always alert to pick up unworn words, ventured to say, perhaps to the astonishment of many, that "there is no speech more energetic, more colored, than that of these people." Balzac was not academic in his vocabulary, and he owed not a little of the sharpness of his descriptions to his hatred of the cut-and-dried phrases of his fellow-novelists. He would willingly have agreed with Montaigne when the essayist declared that the language he liked, written or spoken, was "a succulent and nervous speech, short and compact, not so much delicate and combed out as vehement and brusk, rather arbitrary than monotonous, ... not pedantic, but soldierly rather, as Suetonius called Cæsar's." And this brings us exactly to Mr. Bret Harte's

> Phrases such as camps may teach,
> Saber-cuts of Saxon speech,

There is a more soldierly frankness, a greater freedom, less restraint, less respect for law and order, in the west than in the east; and this may be a reason why American slang is superior to British and to French. The catchwords of New York may be as inept and as cheap as the catchwords of London and of Paris, but New York is not as important to the United States as London is to Great Britain and as Paris is to France; it is not as dominating, not as absorbing. So it is that in America the feebler catchwords of the city give way before the virile phrases of the west. There is little to choose between the *how's your poor feet?* of London and the *well, I should smile* of New York, for neither phrase had any excuse for existence, and neither had any hope of survival. The city phrase is often doubtful in meaning and obscure in origin. In London, for example, the four-wheel cab is called a *growler*. Why? In New York a can brought in filled with beer at a bar-room is called a *growler*, and the act of sending this can from the private house to the public house and back is called *working the growler*. Why?

But when we find a western writer describing the effects of *tanglefoot* whisky, the adjective explains itself, and is justified at once. And we discover immediately the daringly condensed metaphor in the sign, "Don't *monkey* with the *buzz-saw*"; the picturesqueness of the word *buzz-saw* and its fitness for service are visible at a glance. So we understand the phrase readily and appreciate its force when we read the story of 'Buck Fanshaw's Funeral,' and are told that "he never *went back on* his mother," or when we hear the defender of 'Banty Tim' declare that

> "Ef one of you teches the boy
> He'll *wrestle his hash* to-night in hell,
>   Or my name's not Tilman Joy."

To wrestle one's hash is not an elegant expression, one must admit, and it is not likely to be adopted into the literary language; but it is forcible at least, and not stupid. *To go back on*, however, bids fair to take its place in our speech as a phrase at once useful and vigorous.

From the wide and wind-swept plains of the west came *blizzard*, and altho it has been suggested that the word is a survival from some local British dialect, the west still deserves the credit of having rescued it from desuetude. From the logging-camps of the northwest came *boom*, an old word again, but with a new meaning which the language promptly accepted. From still farther west came the use of *sand* to indicate staying power, backbone—what New England knows as *grit* and old England as *pluck* (a far less expressive word). From the southwest came *cinch*, from the tightening of the girths of the pack-mules, and so by extension indicating a grasp of anything so firm that it cannot get away.

Just why a *dead cinch* should be the securest of any, I confess I do not know. *Dead* is here used as an intensive; and the study of intensives is as yet in its infancy. In all parts of Great Britain and the United States we find certain words wrenched from their true meaning and most arbitrarily employed to heighten the value of other words. Thus we have a *dead cinch*, or a *dead sure thing*, a *dead shot*, a *dead level*—and for these last two terms we can discover perhaps a reason. Lowell noted in New England a use of *tormented* as a euphemism for *damned*, as "not a *tormented* cent." Every American traveler in England must have remarked with surprise the British use of the Saxon synonym of *sanguinary* as an intensive, the chief British rivals of *bloody* in this respect being *blooming* and *blasted*. All three are held to be shocking to polite ears, and it was with bated breath that the editor of a London newspaper wrote about the prospects of "a b——y war"; while, as another London editor declared recently, it is now impossible for a cockney to read with proper sympathy Jeffrey's appeal to Carlyle, after a visit to Craigenputtock, to bring his "blooming Eve out of her blasted paradise." Of the other slang synonyms for *very*—*jolly*, "he was *jolly* ill," is British; *awfully* was British first, and is now American also; and *daisy* is American. But any discussion of intensives is a digression here, and I return as soon as may be to the main road.

To freeze to anything or any person is a down-east phrase, so Lowell records, but it has a far-western strength; and so has *to get solid with*, as when the advice is given that "if a man is courting a girl it is best *to get solid with* her father." What is this phrase, however, but the French *solidarité*, which we have recently taken over into English to indicate a communion of interests and responsibilities? The likeness of French terms to American is no new thing; Lowell told us that Horace Mann, in one of his public addresses, commented at some length on the beauty and moral significance of the French phrase *s'orienter*, and called upon his young friends to practise it, altho "there was not a Yankee in his audience whose problem had not always been to find out what was *about east*, and to shape his course accordingly." A few years ago, in turning over 'Karikari,' a volume of M. Ludovic Halévy's clever and charming sketches of Parisian character, I met with a delightful young lady who had *pas pour deux liards de coquetterie*; and I wondered whether M. Halévy, if he were an American, and one of the forty of an American Academy, would venture the assertion that his heroine was *not coquettish for a cent*.

Closely akin to *to freeze to* and *to be solid with* is *jumped on*. When severe reproof is administered the culprit is said to be *jumped on*; and if the reproof shall be unduly severe, the sufferer is said then to be *jumped on with both feet*. All three of these phrases belong to a class from which the literary language has enlisted many worthy recruits in the past, and it would not surprise me to see them answer to their names whenever a new dictionary calls the roll of English words. Will they find themselves shoulder to shoulder with *spook*, a word of Dutch origin, now volunteering for English service both in New York and in South Africa? And by that time will *slump* have been admitted to the ranks, and *fad*, and *crank*, in the secondary meaning of a man of somewhat unsettled mind? *Slump* is an Americanism, *crank* is an Americanism of remote British descent, and *fad* is a Briticism; this last is perhaps the most needed word of the three, and from it we get a name for the *faddist*, the bore who rides his hobby hard and without regard to the hounds.

Just as in New York the "Upper Ten Thousand" of N. P. Willis have shrunk to the "Four Hundred" of Mr. Ward McAllister, so in London the *swells* soon became the *smart* set, and after a while developed into *swagger* people, as they became more and more exclusive and felt the need of new terms to express their new quality. But in no department of speech is the consumption of words more rapid than in that describing the degrees of intoxication; and the list of slang synonyms for the drunkard, and for his condition, and for the act which brings it about, is as long as Leporello's. Among these, *to get loaded* and *to carry a load* are expressions obvious enough; and when we recall that *jag* is a provincialism meaning a light load, we see easily that the man who *has a jag on* is in the earlier stages of intoxication. This use of the word is, I think, wholly American, and it has not crossed the Atlantic as yet, or else a British writer could never have blundered into a definition of *jag* as an umbrella, quoting in illustration a paragraph from a St. Louis paper which said that "Mr. Brown was seen on the street last Sunday in the rain carrying a large fine jag." One may wonder what this British writer would have made out of the remark of the Chicago humorist, that a certain man was not always drunk, even if he did jump "from jag to jag like an alcoholic chamois."

Here, of course, we are fairly within the boundaries of slang—of the slang which is temporary only, and which withers away swiftly. But is *swell* slang now, and *fad*, and *crank*? Is *boom* slang, and is *blizzard*? And if it is difficult to draw any line of division between mere slang on the one side, and idiomatic words and phrases on the other, it is doubly difficult to draw this line between mere slang and the legitimate technicalities of a calling or a craft. Is it slang to say of a picture that the chief figure in it is *out of drawing*, or that the painter has got his *values* wrong? And how could any historian explain the ins and outs of New York politics who could not state frankly that the *machine* made a *slate*, and that the *mugwumps* broke it. Such a historian must needs master the meaning of *laying pipe* for a nomination, or *pulling wires* to secure it, of *taking the stump* before election, and of *log-rolling* after it; he must apprehend the exact relation of the *boss* to his *henchmen* and his *heelers*; and he must understand who the *half-breeds* were, and the *stalwarts*, and how the *swallowtails* were different from the *short-hairs*.

To call one man a *boss* and another a *henchman* may have been slang once, but the words are lawful now, because they are necessary. It is only by these words that the exact relation of a certain kind of political leader to a certain kind of political follower can be expressed succinctly. There are, of course, not a few political phrases still under the ban because they are needless. Some of these may some day come to convey an exact shade of meaning not expressed by any other word, and when this shall happen, they will take their places in the legitimate vocabulary. I doubt whether this good fortune will ever befall a use of *influence,* now not uncommon in Washington. The statesman at whose suggestion and request an office-holder has received his appointment is known as that office-holder's *influence*. Thus a poor widow, suddenly turned out of a post she had held for years, because it was wanted by the henchman of some boss whose good will a senator or a department chief wished to retain, explained to a friend that her dismissal was due to the fact that her *influence* had died during the summer. The inevitable extension of the merit system in the civil service of our country will probably prevent the permanent acceptance of this new meaning.

The political is only one of a vast number of technical vocabularies, all of which are proffering their words for popular consumption. Every art and every science, every trade and every calling, every sect and every sport, has its own special lexicon, the most of the words in which must always remain outside of the general speech of the whole people. They are reserves, to be drawn upon to fill up the regular army in time of need. Legitimate enough when confined to their proper use, those technicalities become slang when employed out of season, and when applied out of the special department of human endeavor in which they have been evolved. Of course, if the public interest in this department is increased for any reason, more and more words from that technical vocabulary are adopted into the wider dictionary of popular speech; and thus the general language is still enriching itself by the taking over of words and phrases from the terminology devised by experts for their own use. Not without interest would it be if we could ascertain exactly how much of the special vocabulary of the mere man of letters is now understandable by the plain people. It is one of the characters in 'Middlemarch' who maintains that "correct English" is only "the slang of prigs who write history and essays, and the strongest slang of all is the slang of poets."

Of recent years many of the locutions of the Stock Exchange have won their way into general knowledge; and there are few of us who do not know what *bears* and *bulls* are, what a *corner* is, and what is a *margin*. The practical application of scientific knowledge makes the public at large familiar with many principles hitherto the exclusive possession of the experts, and the public at large gets to use freely to-day technicalities which even the learned of yesterday would not have understood. *Current*, for example, and *insulation*, made familiar by the startlingly rapid extension of electrical possibilities in the last few years, have been so fully assimilated that they are now used independently and without avowed reference to their original electrical meanings.

The prevalence of a sport or of a game brings into general use the terms of that special amusement. The Elizabethan dramatists, for example, use *vy* and *revy* and the other technicalities of the game of primero as freely as our western humorists use *going it blind* and *calling* and the other technicalities of the game of poker, which has been evolved out of primero in the course of the centuries. Some of the technicalities of euchre also, and of whist, have passed into every-day speech; and so have many of the terms of baseball and of football, of racing and of trotting, of rowing and of yachting. These made their way into the vocabulary of the average man one by one, as the seasons went around and as the sports followed one another in popularity. So during the civil war many military phrases were frequent in the mouths of the people; and some of these established themselves firmly in the vocabulary.

"In language, as in life," so Professor Dowden tells us, "there is, so to speak, an aristocracy and a commonalty: words with a heritage of dignity, words which have been ennobled, and a rabble of words which are excluded from positions of honor and trust." Some writers and speakers there are with so delicate a sense of refinement that they are at ease only with the ennobled words, with the words that came over with the conquerer, with the lords, spiritual and temporal, of the vocabulary. Others there are, parvenus themselves, and so tainted with snobbery that they are happy only in the society of their betters; and these express the utmost contempt for the mass of the vulgar. Yet again others there are who have Lincoln's liking for the plain words of the plain people—the democrats of the dictionary, homely, simple, direct. These last are tolerant of the words, once of high estate, which have lost their rank and are fallen upon evil days, preferring them over the other words, plebeian once, but having pushed their fortunes energetically in successive generations, until now there are none more highly placed.

Perhaps the aristocratic figure of speech is a little misleading, because in the English language, as in France after the Revolution, we find *la carrière ouverte aux talents*, and every word has a fair chance to attain the highest dignity in the gift of the dictionary. No doubt family connections are still potent, and it is much easier for some words to rise in life than it is for others. Most people would hold that war and law and medicine made a more honorable pedigree for a technical term than the stage, for example, or than some sport.

And yet the stage has its own enormous vocabulary, used with the utmost scientific precision. The theater is a hotbed of temporary slang, often as lawless, as vigorous, and as picturesque as the phrases of the west; but it has also a terminology of its own, containing some hundreds of words, used always with absolute exactness. A *mascot*, meaning one who brings good luck, and a *hoodoo*, meaning one who brings ill fortune, are terms invented in the theater, it is true; and many another odd word can be credited to the same source. But every one behind the scenes knows also what *sky-borders* are, and *bunch-lights*, and *vampire-traps*, and *raking-pieces*—technical terms all of them, and all used with rigorous exactitude. Like the technicalities of any other profession, those of the stage are often very puzzling to the uninitiated, and a greenhorn could hardly even make a guess at the meaning of terms which every visitor to a green-room might use at any moment. What layman could explain the office of a *cut-drop*, the utility of a *carpenter's scene*, or the precise privileges of a *bill-board ticket*?

There is one word which the larger vocabulary of the public has lately taken from the smaller vocabulary of the playhouse, and which some strolling player of the past apparently borrowed from some other vagabond familiar with thieves' slang. This word is *fake*. It has always conveyed the suggestion of an intent to deceive. "Are you going to get up new scenery for the new play?" might be asked; and the answer would be, "No; we shall *fake* it," meaning thereby that old scenery would be retouched and readjusted so as to have the appearance of new. From the stage the word passed to the newspapers, and a *fake* is a story invented, not founded on fact, "made out of whole cloth," as the stump-speakers say. Mr. Howells, always bold in using new words, accepts *fake* as good enough for him, and prints it in the 'Quality of Mercy' without the stigma of italics or quotation-marks; just as in the same story he has adopted the colloquial *electrics* for *electric lights*—i.e., "He turned off the electrics."

And hereafter the rest of us may use either *fake* or *electrics* with a clear conscience, either hiding ourselves behind Mr. Howells, who can always give a good account of himself when attacked, or else coming out into the open and asserting our own right to adopt either word because it is useful. "Is it called for? Is it accordant with the analysis of the language? Is it offered or backed by good authority? These are the considerations by which general consent is won or repelled," so Professor Whitney tells us, "and general consent decides every case without appeal." It happens that Don Quixote preceded Professor Whitney in this exposition of the law, for when he was instructing Sancho Panza, then about to be appointed governor of an island, he used a Latinized form of a certain word which had become vulgar, explaining that "if some do not understand these terms it matters little, for custom will bring them into use in the course of time so that they will be readily understood. That is the way a language is enriched; custom and the public are all-powerful there." Sometimes the needful word which is thought to be too common for use is Latinized, as Don Quixote preferred, but more often it is ennobled without change, being simply lifted out from among its former low companions.

One of the hardest lessons for the amateurs in linguistics to learn—and most of them never attain to this wisdom—is that affectations are fleeting, that vulgarisms die of their own weakness, and that corruptions do little harm to the language. And the reason is not far to seek: either the apparent affectation, the alleged vulgarism, the so-called corruption, is accidental and useless, in which case its vogue will be brief and it will sink swiftly into oblivion; or else it represents a need and fills a want, in which case, no matter how careless it may be or how inaccurately formed, it will hold its own firmly, and there is really nothing more to be said about it. In other words, slang and all other variations from the high standard of the literary language are either temporary or permanent. If they are temporary only, the damage they can do is inconsiderable. If they are permanent, their survival is due solely to the fact that they were convenient or necessary. When a word or a phrase has come to stay (as *reliable* has, apparently), it is idle to denounce a decision rendered by the court of last resort. The most that we can do with advantage is to refrain from using the word ourselves, if we so prefer.

It is possible to go further, even, and to turn the tables on those who see in slang an ever-growing evil. Not only is there little danger to the language to be feared from those alleged corruptions, and from these doubtful locutions of evanescent popularity, but real harm is done by the purists themselves, who do not understand every modification of our language, and who seek to check the development of idiom and to limit the liberty which enables our speech freely to provide for its own needs as these are revealed by time. It is these half-educated censors, prompt to protest against whatever is novel to them, and swift to set up the standard of a narrow personal experience, who try to curb the development of a language. It cannot be declared too often and too emphatically how fortunate it is that the care of our language and the control of its development is not in the hands even of the most competent scholars. In language, as in politics, the people at large are in the long run better judges of their own needs than any specialist can be. As Professor Whitney says, "the language would soon be shorn of no small part of its strength if placed exclusively in the hands of any individual or of any class." In the hands of no class would it be enfeebled sooner than if it were given to the guardianship of the pedants and the pedagogs.

A sloven in speech is as offensive as a sloven in manners or in dress; and neatness of phrase is as pleasant to the ear as neatness of attire to the eye. A man should choose his words at least as carefully as he chooses his clothes; a hint of the dandy even is unobjectionable, if it is but a hint. But when a man gives his whole mind to his dress, it is generally because he has but little mind to give; and so when a man spends his force wholly in rejecting words and phrases, it is generally because he lacks ideas to express with the words and phrases of which he does approve. In most cases a man can say best what he has to say without lapsing into slang; but then a slangy expression which actually tells us something is better than the immaculate sentence empty of everything but the consciousness of its own propriety.

(1893)

IX
QUESTIONS OF USAGE

If any proof were needed of the fact that an immense number of people take an intense interest in the right and wrong use of the English language, and also of the further fact that their interest is out of all proportion to their knowledge of the history of our speech, such proof could be found in the swift and unceasing eruption of "letters to the editor" which broke out in many of the American newspapers immediately after the publication of Mr. Rudyard Kipling's 'Recessional.' The exciting cause of this rash exhibition was found in the line which told us that

> The shouting and the tumult dies.

The gross blunder in this sentence leaped to the eyes of many whose acquaintance with the principles of English construction was confined to what they chanced to remember of the rules learned by heart in their grammar-school days. But there were others whose reading was a little wider, and who were able to cite precedents in Mr. Kipling's favor from Milton and from Shakspere and from the King James translation of the Bible. Yet the argument from the past failed to convince some of the original protestants, one of whom suggested that the erring poet should be sent to a night-school, while another objected to any further discussion of the subject, since "a person who doesn't know that the plural form of the verb is used when the subject of said verb is two or more nouns in the singular number should receive no mention in a reputable newspaper." It may be doubted whether the altercation was really bloody enough to demand attention from the disreputable newspapers, altho it was fierce and intolerant while it lasted.

The battle raged for a fortnight, and the foundations of the deep were broken up. Yet it was really a tempest in a teapot, and oil for the troubled waters was ready at hand had any of those in danger of shipwreck thought to make use of it. In Professor Lounsbury's 'History of the English Language'—a book from which it is a constant pleasure to quote, since it combines sound scholarship, literary skill, and common sense in an uncommon degree—we are told that "rules have been and still are laid down ... which never had any existence outside of the minds of grammarians and verbal critics. By these rules, so far as they are observed, freedom of expression is cramped, idiomatic peculiarity destroyed, and false tests for correctness set up, which give the ignorant opportunity to point out supposed error in others, while the real error lies in their own imperfect acquaintance with the best usage."

And then Professor Lounsbury cites in illustration the rule which was brought up against Mr. Kipling: "There is a rule of Latin syntax that two or more substantives joined by a copulative require the verb to be in the plural. This has been foisted into the grammar of English, of which it is no more true than it is of modern German.... The grammar of English, as exhibited in the utterances of its best writers and speakers, has from the very earliest period allowed the widest discretion as to the use either of the singular or the plural in such cases. The importation and imposition of rules foreign to its idiom, like the one just mentioned, does more to hinder the free development of the tongue, and to dwarf its freedom of expression, than the widest prevalence of slovenliness of speech, or of affectation of style; for these latter are always temporary in their character, and are sure to be left behind by the advance in popular cultivation, or forgotten through the change in popular taste."

This is really a declaration of independence for writers of English. It is the frank assertion that a language is made by those who use it—made by that very use. Language is not an invention of the grammarians and of the word-critics, whose business, indeed, is not to make language or to prescribe rules, but more modestly to record usage and to discover the principles which may underlie the incessant development of our common speech. And here in discussing the syntax Professor Lounsbury is at one with Mr. George Meredith discussing the vocabulary of our language, when the British novelist notes his own liking for "our blunt and racy vernacular, which a society nourished upon Norman English and English Latin banishes from print, largely to its impoverishment, some think."

Those who have tried to impose a Latin syntax on the English language are as arbitrary as those who have insisted on an English pronunciation of the Latin language. Their attitude is as illogical as it is dogmatic; and nowhere is dogmatism less welcome than in the attempt to come to a just conclusion in regard to English usage; and nowhere is the personal equation more carefully to be allowed for. A term is not necessarily acceptable because we ourselves are accustomed to it, nor is it necessarily to be rejected because it reaches us as a novelty. The Americanism which a British journalist glibly denounces may be but the ephemeral catchword of a single street-gang, or it may have come over in the 'Mayflower' and be able to trace its ancestry back to a forefather that crossed with William the Conqueror. The Briticism which strikes some of us as uncouth and vulgar may be but a chance bit of cockney slang, or it may be warranted by the very genius of our language.

Most of the little manuals which pretend to regulate our use of our own language and to declare what is and what is not good English are grotesque in their ignorance; and the best of them are of small value, because they are prepared on the assumption that the English language is dead, like the Latin, and that, like Latin again, its usage is fixed finally. Of course this assumption is as far as possible from the fact. The English language is alive now—very much alive. And because it is alive it is in a constant state of growth. It is developing daily according to its needs. It is casting aside words and usages that are no longer satisfactory; it is adding new terms as new things are brought forward; and it is making new usages, as convenience suggests, short-cuts across lots, and to the neglect of the five-barred gates rigidly set up by our ancestors. It is throwing away as worn out words which were once very fashionable; and it is giving up grammatical forms which seem to be no longer useful. It is continually trying to keep itself in the highest state of efficiency for work it has to do. It is ever urging ahead in the direction of increased utility; and if any of the so-called "rules" happens to stand in the path of its progress—so much the worse for the rule! As Stephenson said, "It will be bad for the coo!"

The English language is the tool of the peoples who speak English and who have made it to fit their hands. They have fashioned it to suit their own needs, and it is quite as characteristic as anything else these same peoples have made—quite as characteristic as the common law and as parliamentary government. A language cannot but be a most important witness when we wish to inquire into the special peculiarities of a race. The French, for instance, are dominated by the social instinct, and they are prone to rely on logic a little too much, and their language is therefore a marvel of transparency and precision. In like manner we might deduce from an analysis of the German language an opinion as to the slowness of the individual Teuton, as to his occasional cloudiness, as to his willingness to take trouble, and as to his ultimate thoroughness.

The peoples who speak English are very practical and very direct; they are impatient of needless detail; and they are intolerant of mere theory. These are some of the reasons why English is less embarrassed with niceties of inflection than other languages, why it has cut its syntax to the bone, why it has got rid of most of its declensions and conjugations—why, in short, it has almost justified the critic who called it a grammarless tongue. In every language there is a constant tendency toward uniformity and an unceasing effort to get rid of abnormal exceptions to the general rule; but in no language are these endeavors more effective than in English. In the past they have succeeded in simplifying the rules of our speech; and they are at work now in the present on the same task of making English a more efficient instrument for those who use it.

This effort of the language to do its duty as best it can is partly conscious and partly unconscious; and where the word-critic can be of service is in watching for the result of the unconscious endeavor, so that it can be made plain, and so that it can be aided thereafter by conscious endeavor. The tendency toward uniformity is irresistible; and one of its results just now to be observed is an impending disappearance of the subjunctive mood. Those who may have supposed that the subjunctive was as firmly established in English as the indicative can discover easily enough by paying a little attention to their own daily speech and to the speech of their educated neighbors that "if I *be* not too late," for instance, is a form now rarely heard even in cultivated society.

And the same tendency is to be observed also in the written language. Letters in the London *Author* in June and July, 1897, showed that in a few less than a million words chosen from the works of recent authors of good repute there were only 284 instances of the subjunctive mood, and that of these all but fifteen were in the verb "to be." This reveals to us that the value of this variation of form is no longer evident, not merely to careless speakers, but even to careful writers; and it makes it probable that it is only a question of time how soon the subjunctive shall be no longer differentiated from the indicative. Where our grandfathers would have taken pains to say "if I *were* to go away," and "if I *be* not misinformed," our grandchildren will unhesitatingly write, "if I *was* to go away," and "if I *am* not misinformed." And so posterity will not need to clog its memory with any rule for the employment of the subjunctive; and the English language will have cleansed itself of a barnacle.

It is this same irresistible desire for the simplest form and for the shortest which is responsible for the increasing tendency to say "he don't" and "she don't," on the analogy of "we don't," "you don't," and "they don't," instead of the more obviously grammatical "he does n't" and "she does n't." A brave attempt has been made to maintain that "he don't" is older than "he does n't," and that it has at least the sanction of antiquity. However this may be, "he don't" is certain to sustain itself in the future because it calls for less effort and because any willingness to satisfy the purist will seem less and less worth while as time goes on. It is well that the purist should fight for his own hand; but it is well also to know that he is fighting a losing battle.

The purist used to insist that we should not say "the house is *being built*," but rather "the house is *building*." So far as one can judge from a survey of recent writing the purist has abandoned this combat; and nobody nowadays hesitates to ask, "What is being done?" The purist still objects to what he calls the Retained Object in such a sentence as "he was given a new suit of clothes." Here again the struggle is vain, for this usage is very old; it is well established in English; and whatever may be urged against it theoretically, it has the final advantage of convenience. The purist also tells us that we should say "come to see me" and "try to do it," and not "come and see me" and "try and do it." Here once more the purist is setting up a personal standard without any warrant. He may use whichever of these forms he likes best, and we on our part have the same permission, with a strong preference for the older and more idiomatic of them.

Theory is all very well, but to be of any value it must be founded on the solid rock of fact; and even when it is so established it has to yield to convenience. This is what the purist cannot be induced to understand. He seems to think that the language was made once for all, and that any deviation from the theory acted on in the past is intolerable in the present. He is often wholly at sea in regard to his theories and to his facts—more often than not; but no doubt as to his own infallibility ever discourages him. He just knows that he is right and that everybody else is wrong; and he has no sense of humor to save him from himself. And he makes up in violence what he lacks in wisdom. He accepts himself as a prophet verbally inspired, and he holds that this gives him the right to call down fire from heaven on all who do not accept his message.

It was a purist of this sort who once wrote to a little literary weekly in New York, protesting against the use of *people* when *persons* would seem to be the better word, and complacently declaring that "for twenty-five years or more I have kept my eye on this little word *people* and I have yet to find a single American or English author who does not misuse it." We are instantly reminded of the Irish juryman who said, "Eleven more obstinate men I never met in the whole course of my life." In this pitiful condition of affairs one cannot discover on what this purist bases the hope he expresses that "in the course of two or three hundred years the correct employment of it may possibly become general." Rather may it be hoped that in the course of two or three hundred years a knowledge of the principles which govern English usage may become general.

What is called the Split Infinitive is also a cause of pain to the purist, who is greatly grieved when he finds George Lewes in the 'Life of Goethe' saying "to completely understand." This inserting of an adverb between the *to* and the rest of the verb strikes the word-critic as pernicious, and he denounces it instantly as a novelty to be stamped out before it permanently contaminates our speech. Even Professor A. S. Hill, in his 'Foundations of Rhetoric,' while admitting its antiquity, since it has been in use constantly from the days of Wyclif to the days of Herbert Spencer, still declares it to be "a common fault" not sanctioned or even condoned by good authority.

The fact is, I think, that the Split Infinitive has a most respectable pedigree, and that it is rather the protest against it which is the novelty now establishing itself. The Split Infinitive is to be found in the pages of Shakspere, Massinger, Sir Thomas Browne, Defoe, Burke, Coleridge, Byron, De Quincey, Macaulay, Matthew Arnold, Browning, Motley, Lowell, and Holmes. But it is a fact also, I think, that since the protest has been raised there has been a tendency among careful writers to eschew the Split Infinitive, or at least to employ it only when there is a gain in lucidity from its use, as there is, for example, in Professor Lounsbury's "to more than counterbalance" ('Studies in Chaucer,' i. 447).

A writer who has worked out for himself a theory of style, and who has made up his mind as to the principles he ought to follow in writing, often yields to protests the validity of which he refuses to admit. He gives the protestant the benefit of the doubt and drops the stigmatized words from his vocabulary and refrains from the stigmatized usages, reserving always the right to avail himself of them at a pinch. What such a writer has for his supreme object is to convey his thought into the minds of his readers with the least friction; and he tries therefore to avoid all awkwardness of phrase, all incongruous words, all locutions likely to arouse resistance, since any one of these things will inevitably lessen the amount of attention which this reader or that will then have available for the reception of the writer's message. This is what Herbert Spencer has called the principle of Economy of Attention; and a firm grasp of this principle is a condition precedent to a clear understanding of literary art.

For a good and sufficient reason such a writer stands ready at any time to break this self-imposed rule. If a solecism, or a vulgarism even, will serve his purpose better at a given moment than the more elegant word, he avails himself of it, knowing what he is doing, and risking the smaller loss for the greater gain. M. Legouvé tells us that at a rehearsal of a play of Scribe's he drew the author's attention to a bit of bad French at the climax of one of the acts, and Scribe gratefully accepted the correct form which was suggested. But two or three rehearsals later Scribe went back unhesitatingly to the earlier and incorrect phrase, which happened to be swifter, more direct, and dramatically more expressive than the academically accurate sentence M. Legouvé had supplied. Shakspere seems often to have been moved by like motives, and to have been willing at any time to sacrifice strict grammar to stage-effectiveness.

Two tendencies exist side by side to-day, and are working together for the improvement of our language. One is the tendency to disregard all useless distinctions and to abolish all useless exceptions and to achieve simplicity and regularity. The other is the tendency toward a more delicate precision which shall help the writer to present his thought with the utmost clearness.

Of the first of these abundant examples can be cited phrases which the word-critic would denounce, and which are not easy to defend on any narrow ground, but which are employed freely even by conscientious writers, well aware that no utility is served by a pedantic precision. So we find Matthew Arnold in his lectures 'On Translating Homer' speaking of "the *four first*," where the purist would prefer to have said "the *first four*." So we find Hawthorne in the 'Blithedale Romance' writing "fellow, clown, or bumpkin, to *either* of these," when the purist would have wished him to say "to any one of these," holding that "either" can be applied only when there are but two objects.

In like manner the word-critics object to the use of the superlative degree when the comparative is all that is needed; yet we find in the King James translation of Genesis, "her eldest son, Esau," and she had but two sons. And they refuse to allow either a comparative or a superlative to adjectives which indicate completeness; yet we find in Gibbon's 'Decline and Fall,' "its success was not more universal." They do not like to see a writer say that anything is "more perfect" or "most complete," holding that what is universal or perfect or complete "does not admit of augmentation," as one of them declared more than a century ago in the *Gentleman's Magazine* for July, 1797. In all these cases logic may be on the side of the word-critic. But what of it? Obedience to logic would here serve no useful purpose, and therefore logic is boldly disobeyed. However inexact these phrases may be, they mislead no one and they can be understood without hesitation.

Side by side with this tendency to take the short-cut exists the other tendency to go the long way round if by so doing the writer's purpose is more easily accomplished. There is a common usage which is frequently objurgated by the word-critics and which may fall into desuetude, not through their attacks, but because of its conflict with this second tendency. This is the insertion of an unnecessary *who* or *which* after an *and* or a *but*, as in this sentence from Professor Butcher's admirable discussion of Aristotle's 'Theory of Poetry': "Nature is an artist capable indeed of mistakes, but *who* by slow advances and through many failures realizes her own idea." So in Gibbon's 'Decline and Fall' we are told of "a chorus of twenty-seven youths and as many virgins, of noble family, and *whose* parents were both alive." This locution is proper in French, but it is denounced as improper in English by the purists, who would strike out the *but* from Professor Butcher's and the *and* from Gibbon's.

It is a constant source of amusement to those interested in observing the condition and the development of the language to note the frequency with which the phrases put under taboo by the word-critics occur in the writings of the masters of English. In my own recent reading I have found this despised construction in the pages of Fielding, Johnson, Thackeray, Matthew Arnold, Robert Louis Stevenson, Mr. John Morley, Mr. Henry James, and Professor Jebb in Great Britain, and in pages of Hawthorne, Lowell, Holmes, and Mr. John Fiske in the United States. What is more significant perhaps is its discovery in the works of professed students of language—Trench, Isaac Taylor, Max Müller, and W. D. Whitney.

And yet, in spite of this array of authorities, I am inclined to believe that this usage may perhaps disappear with the increasing attention which the best writers are now giving to the rhythm and balance of their sentences. It is not that the form is wrong—that is a matter not to be decided offhand; it is that the form is awkward and that it jars on the feeling for symmetry—the feeling which leads us to put a candlestick on each side of the clock on the mantelpiece. Professor Whitney began one of his sentences thus: "Castrén, himself a Finn, and whose long and devoted labors have taught us more respecting them than has been brought to light by any other man, ventures," etc. Would not this sentence have been easier and more elegant if Whitney had either struck out *and* (which is not needed at all) or else inserted *who was* after Castrén? In the sentence as Whitney wrote it *and whose* makes me look back for the *who* which my feeling for symmetry leads me to suppose must have preceded it somewhere, and in this vain search part of my attention is abstracted. I have been forced to think of the manner of his remarks when my mind ought to have given itself so far as might be to the matter of them. In other words, the real objection to this usage is that it is in violation of the principle of Economy of Attention.

Another usage also under fire from the purists is exemplified in another extract from Whitney: "It is, I am convinced, a mistake to commence at once upon a course of detailed comparative philology with pupils who have *only* enjoyed the ordinary training in the classical or modern languages." Obviously his meaning would be more sharply defined if he had put *only* after instead of before *enjoyed*. So Froude, writing about 'English Seamen in the Sixteenth Century,' says that "the fore-and-aft rig alone would enable a vessel to tack, as it is called, and this could *only* be used with craft of moderate tonnage"; and here again a transposition after the verb would increase the exactness of the statement.

The proposition of *only* is really important only when the misplacing of it may cause ambiguity; and Professor F. N. Scott has shown how Webster, always careful in the niceties of style, unhesitatingly put *only* out of its proper place, if by so doing he could improve the rhythm of his period, as in this sentence from the second Bunker Hill oration: "It did not, indeed, put an end to the war; but, in the then existing hostile state of feeling, the difficulties could only be referred to the arbitration of the sword." This is as it should be, the small effect promptly sacrificed for the larger. The rule—if rule it really is—must be broken unhesitatingly when there is greater gain than loss.

There is an anecdote in some volume of French theatrical memoirs narrating an experience of Mademoiselle Clairon, the great tragic actress, with a pupil of hers, a girl of fine natural gifts for the histrionic art, but far too frequent and too exuberant in her gesticulation. So when the pupil was once to appear before the public in a recitation, Mademoiselle Clairon bound the girl's arms to her side by a stiff thread and sent her thus upon the stage. With the first strong feeling she had to express the pupil tried to raise her arms, only to be restrained by the thread. A dozen times in the course of her recitation she was prevented from making the gestures she desired, until at the very end she could stand it no longer, and in the climax of her emotion she broke her bonds and lifted her hands to her head. When she came off the stage she went humbly to where Mademoiselle Clairon was standing in the wings and apologized for having snapped the thread. "But you did quite right!" said the teacher. "That was the time to make the gesture—not before!"

Rules exist to aid in composition; and by wise men composition is not undertaken merely to prove the existence of the rules. Circumstances may alter even codes of manners; in Paris, for instance, it is permissible to sop bread in the sauce, a practice which is bad form in London—since nobody would want any more of a British sauce than could be avoided. This paper, however, has failed of its purpose if it is taken as a plea for license. Rather is it intended as an argument for liberty. It has been written as the result of a belief that a frank protest is needed now and again against the excessive demands of the linguistic dogmatists. That what the linguistic dogmatists write is as widely read as it seems to be is a sign of a healthy interest in the speech which must serve us all, scholars and school-masters and plain people. This interest should be aroused also to shake off the shackles with which pedagogs and pedants seek to restrain not only the full growth of our noble tongue, but even its free use. As Renan pithily put it, every time that "grammarians have tried deliberately to reform a language, they have succeeded only in making it heavy, without expression, and often less logical than the humblest dialect."

If English is to be kept fit to do the mighty work it bids fair to be called upon to accomplish in the future, it must be allowed to develop along the line of least resistance. It must be encouraged to follow its own bent and to supply its own needs and to shed its worn-out members. It must not be hampered by syntax taken from Latin or by rules evolved out of the inner consciousness of word-critics. It must not be too squeamish or even too particular, since excessive refinement goes only with muscular weakness. It must be allowed to venture on solecisms, on neologisms, on Americanisms, on Briticisms, on Australianisms, if need be, however ugly some of these may seem, for the language uses itself up fast, and has to be replenished that it shall not lose its vigor and its ardor.

To say this is not to say that every one of us who uses English in speaking or in writing should not always choose his words carefully and decide on his forms judiciously. Only by a wise selection can the language be kept at its highest efficiency; only thus can its full powers be revealed to us. And if we decide that we prefer to keep to the very letter of the law as laid down by the grammarians—why, that is our privilege and no one shall say us nay. But let us not think scorn of those who are careless in paying their tithes of mint and anise and cummin, if also they stand upright and speak the truth plainly.

For myself—if a personal confession is not here out of place—I shrink always from profiting by any license I have just claimed for others; I strive always to eschew the Split Infinitive, to avoid *and who* when there is no preceding *who* which may balance it, and to put *only* always in the place where it will do most good. It is ever my aim to avail myself of the phrase which will convey my meaning into the reader's mind with the least friction; and out of the effort to achieve this approach along the line of least resistance, I get something of the joy an honest craftsman ought always to feel in the handling of his tools. For this is what words are, after all; they are the tools of man, devised to serve his daily needs. As Bagehot once suggested, we may not know how language was first invented and made, "but beyond doubt it was shaped and fashioned into its present state by common, ordinary men and women using it for common and ordinary purposes. They wanted a carving-knife, not a razor or lancet; and those great artists who have to use language for more exquisite purposes, who employ it to describe changing sentiments and momentary fancies and the fluctuating and indefinite inner world, must use curious nicety and hidden but effectual artifice, else they cannot duly punctuate their thoughts and slice the fine edges of their reflections. A hair's breadth is as important to them as a yard's breadth to a common workman."

(1898)

X
AN INQUIRY AS TO RIME

"I have a theory about double rimes for which I shall be attacked by the critics, but which I could justify perhaps on high authority, or, at least, analogy," wrote Mrs. Browning to a friend not long after the publication of one of her books. "These volumes of mine have more double rimes than any two books of English poems that ever to my knowledge were printed; I mean of English poems not comic. Now of double rimes in use which are perfect rimes you are aware how few there are; and yet you are also aware of what an admirable effect in making a rhythm various and vigorous double riming is in English poetry. Therefore I have used a certain license; and after much thoughtful study of the Elizabethan writers have ventured it with the public. And do you tell me—you who object to the use of a different vowel in a double rime—why you rime (as everybody does, without blame from everybody) *given* to *heaven*, when you object to my riming *remember* to *chamber*? The analogy is all on my side, and I believe that the spirit of the English language is also."

Here Mrs. Browning raises a question of interest to all who have paid any attention to the technic of verse. No doubt double rimes do give vigor and variety to a poem, altho no modern English lyrist has really rivaled the magnificent medieval 'Dies Iræ,' wherein the double rimes thrice repeated fall one after the other like the beating of mighty trip-hammers. There is no doubt also that the English language is not so fertile in double rimes as the Latin, the German, or the Italian; and that some of the English poets, clutching for these various and vigorous effects, have refused to abide by the strict letter of the law, and have claimed the license of modifying the emphatic vowel from one line to another. Mrs. Browning defends this revolt, and finds it easy to retort to her correspondent that he himself has ventured to link *heaven* and *given*. Many another poet has coupled these unwilling words; and not a few have also married *river* and *ever*, *meadow* and *shadow*, *spirit* and *inherit*.

Mrs. Browning is prepared to justify herself by authority, or at least by analogy; and yet, in bringing about the espousal of *chamber* and *remember*, she is evidently aware that it is no love-match she is aiding and abetting, but at best a marriage of convenience. She pleads precedence to excuse her infraction of a statute the general validity of which she apparently admits. The most that she claims is that the tying together of *chamber* and *remember* is permissible. She seems to say that these ill-mated pairs are, of course, not the best possible rimes, but that, since double rimes are scarce in English, the lyrist may, now and then, avail himself of the second best. An American poet of my acquaintance is bolder than the British poetess; he has the full courage of his convictions. He assures me that he takes pleasure in the tying together of incompatible words like *river* and *ever, meadow* and *shadow*, finding in these arbitrary matings a capricious and agreeable relief from the monotony of more regular riming.

This forces us to consider the basis upon which any theory of "allowable" rimes must rest—any theory, that is, which, after admitting that certain rimes are exact and absolutely adequate, asserts also that certain other combinations of terminal words, altho they do not rime completely and to the satisfaction of all, are still tolerable. This theory accepts certain rimes as good, and it claims in addition certain others as "good enough."

Any objection to the pairing of *spirit* and *inherit*, of *remember* and *chamber*, and the like, cannot be founded upon the fact that in the accepted orthography of the English language the spelling of the terminations differs. Rime has to do with pronunciation and not with orthography; rime is a match between sounds. The symbols that represent these sounds—or that may misrepresent them more or less violently—are of little consequence. What is absurdly called a "rime to the eye" is a flagrant impossibility, or else *hiccough* may pair off with *enough, clean* with *ocean,* and *plague* with *ague.* The eye is not the judge of sound, any more than the nose is the judge of color. *Height* is not a rime to *eight*; but it is a rime to *sight,* to *bite,* to *proselyte,* and to *indict.* So *one* does not rime with either *gone* or *tone*; but it does with *son* and with *bun. Tomb* and *comb,* and *rhomb* and *bomb* are not rimes; but *tomb* and *doom,* and *spume* and *rheum* are. The objection to the linking together of *meadow* and *shadow,* and of *ever* and *river* is far deeper than any superficial difference of spelling; it is rooted in the difference of the sounds themselves. In spite of the invention of printing, or even of writing itself, the final appeal of poetry is still to the ear and not to the eye.

Probably the first utterances of man were rhythmic, and probably poetry had advanced far toward perfection long before the alphabet was devised as an occasional substitute for speech. In the beginning the poet had to charm the ears of those whom he sought to move, since there was then no way by which he could reach the eye also. To the rhapsodists verse was an oral art solely, as it is always for the dramatists, whose speeches must fall trippingly from the tongue, or fail of their effect. The work of the lyrist—writer of odes, minnesinger, troubadour, ballad-minstrel—has always been intended to be said or sung; that it should be read is an afterthought only. Even to-day, when the printing-press has us all under its wheels, it is by our tongues that we possess ourselves of the poetry we truly relish. A poem is not really ours till we know it by heart and can say it to ourselves, or at least until we have read it aloud, and until we can quote it freely. If a poem has actually taken hold on our souls, it rings in our ears, even if we happen to be visualizers also, and can call up at will the printed page whereon it is preserved.

This fact, that poetry is primarily meant to be spoken aloud rather than read silently, altho obvious when plainly stated, has not been firmly grasped by many of those who have considered the technic of the art, and therefore there is often obscurity in the current discussions of rime and rhythm. In the rhetoric of verse there is to-day not a little of the confusion which existed in the rhetoric of prose before Herbert Spencer put forth his illuminating and stimulating essay on the 'Philosophy of Style.' Even in that paper he suggested that the principle of Economy of Attention was as applicable to verse as to prose; and he remarked that "were there space, it might be worth while to inquire whether the pleasure we take in rime, and also that which we take in euphony, are not partly ascribable to the same general cause."

This principle of Economy of Attention explains why it is that any style of speaking or writing is more effective than another, by reminding us that we have, at any given moment, only so much power of attention, and that, therefore, however much of this power has to be employed on the form of any message must be subtracted from the total power, leaving just so much less attention available for the apprehension of the message itself. To convey a thought from one mind to another, we must use words the reception of which demands more or less mental exertion; and therefore that statement is best which carries the thought with the least verbal friction. Some friction there must be always; but the less there is, the more power of attention the recipient has left to master the transmitted thought.

It is greatly to be regretted that Spencer did not spare the space to apply to verse this principle, which has been so helpful in the analysis of prose. He did go so far as to suggest that metrical language is more effective than prose, because when "we habitually preadjust our perceptions to the measured movement of verse" it is "probable that by so doing we economize attention." This suggestion has been elaborated by one of his disciples, the late Mr. Grant Allen, in his treatise on 'Physiological Esthetics,' and it has been formally controverted by the late Mr. Gurney, in his essay on the 'Power of Sound.' Perhaps both Spencer and Gurney are right; part of our pleasure in rhythm is due to the fact that "the mind may economize its energies by anticipating the attention required for each syllable," as the former says, and part of it is "of an entirely positive kind, acting directly on the sense," as the latter maintains.

Whether or not Spencer's principle of Economy of Attention adequately explains our delight in rhythm, there is no doubt that it can easily be utilized to construct a theory of rime. Indeed, it is the one principle which provides a satisfactory solution to the problem propounded by Mrs. Browning. No one can deny that more or less of our enjoyment of rimed verse is due to the skill with which the poet satisfies with the second rime the expectation he has aroused with the first. When he ends a line with *gray*, or *grow*, or *grand*, we do not know which of the twoscore or more of possible rimes to each of these the lyrist will select, and we await his choice with happy anticipation. If he should balk us of our pleasure, if he should omit the rime we had confidently counted upon, we are rudely awakened from our dream of delight, and we ask ourselves abruptly what has happened. It is as tho the train of thought had run off the track. Spencer notes how we are put out by halting versification; "much as at the bottom of a flight of stairs a step more or less than we counted upon gives us a shock, so too does a misplaced accent or a supernumerary syllable."

So, too, does an inaccurate or an arbitrary rime give us a shock. If verse is something to be said or sung, if its appeal is to the ear primarily, if rime is a terminal identity of sound, then any theory of "allowable" rimes is impossible, since an "allowable" rime is necessarily inexact, and thus may tend to withdraw attention from the matter of the poem to its manner. No doubt there are readers who do not notice the incompatibility of these matings, and there are others who notice yet do not care. But the more accurately trained the ear is, the more likely these alliances are to annoy; and the less exact the rime, the more likely the ear is to discover the discrepancy. The only safety for the rimester who wishes to be void of all offense is to risk no union of sounds against whose marriage anybody knows any just cause of impediment. Perhaps a wedding within the prohibited degrees may be allowed to pass without protest now and again; but sooner or later somebody will surely forbid the banns.

Just as a misplaced accent or a supernumerary syllable gives us a shock, so does the attempt of Mrs. Browning to pair off *remember* and *chamber*; so may also the attempt of Poe to link together *valleys* and *palace*. The lapse from the perfect ideal may be but a trifle, but a lapse it is nevertheless. A certain percentage of our available attention may thus be wasted, and worse than wasted; it may be called away from the poem itself, and absorbed suddenly by the mere versification. For a brief moment we may be forced to consider a defect of form, when we ought to have our minds absolutely free to receive the poet's meaning. Whenever a poet cheats us of our expectancy of perfect rime, he forces us to pay exorbitant freight charges on the gift he has presented to us.

It is to be noted, however, that as rime is a matching of sounds, certain pairs of words whose union is not beyond reproach can hardly be rejected without pedantry, since the ordinary pronunciation of cultivated men takes no account of the slight differences of sound audible if the words are uttered with absolute precision. Thus Tennyson in the 'Revenge' rimes *Devon* and *Heaven*; and thus Lowell in the 'Fable for Critics' rimes *irresistible* and *untwistable*. In 'Elsie Venner' Dr. Holmes held up to derision "the inevitable rime of cockney and Yankee beginners, *morn* and *dawn*"; but, at the risk of revealing myself as a Yankee of New York, I must confess that any pronunciation of this pair of words seems to me stilted that does not make them quite impeccable as a rime.

We are warned, however, to be on our guard against pushing any principle to an absurd extreme. If certain pairs of words have been sent forth into the world by English poets from a time whereof the memory of man runneth not to the contrary, then perhaps they may now plead prescription whenever any cold-hearted commentator is disposed to doubt the legitimacy of their conjunction. Altho the union is forbidden by the strict letter of the law,—like marriage with a deceased wife's sister in England,—only the censorious are disposed to take the matter into court. In time certain rimes—falsely so called—"are legitimated by custom," one British critic has declared, citing *love* and *prove*, for example, and asserting that "*river* has just got to rime with *ever* or the game cannot be played." You must have *forgiven* or you will never get to *heaven*. "We expect these licenses and do not resent them, as we do resent Poe's *valleys* and *palace* and the eccentricities of Mrs. Browning." That there is force in this contention cannot be denied; but it must be remembered that those who urge it are necessarily lovers of poetry, or at least fairly familiar with a large body of English verse, or else they would not be aware of the fact that *love* and *prove*, *heaven* and *given*, have often been tied together. But even if these critics, who have been sophisticated by over-familiarity with poetic license, do not resent this pairing of unequal sounds, it does not follow that those who for the first time hear *dove* linked with *Jove* are equally forgiving or negligent. Even if these licenses are pardoned by some as venial offenses, there are others whose ears are annoyed by them and whose attention is distracted. In other words, we are here face to face with the personal equation; and the only way for a writer of verse to be certain that one or another of his rimes will not be resented by this reader or that is to make sure that all his marriages are flawless.

Thus and thus only can he avoid offense with absolute certainty. If his rimes are perfect to the ear when read aloud or recited, then they will never divert the attention of the auditor from the matter of the poem to the mere manner. On the other hand, it is only fair to confess that there are some lovers of poetry who find a charm in lawlessness and in eccentricity. A series of perfect rimes pleases them; but so also does an occasional rime in which the vowel is slightly varied. And the poet's consolation for the loss of these must lie in the knowledge that he cannot hope to satisfy everybody. Consolation may lie also in the belief that any lapse from the perfect rime is dangerous, for even if there are some who enjoy the divergence when it is delicate,—that is, when the vowel sound, even if not absolutely identical, is sympathetically akin,—there are very few who are not annoyed when the difference becomes as obvious as in the attempt to link together *dial* and *ball* or *water* and *clear*.

And as it is only a sophisticated ear which enjoys the mating of *valleys* with *palace*, for example, so the attempted rime of this type is to be found chiefly in the more labored poets—in those who are consciously literary. The primitive lyrist, the unconscious singer who makes a ballad of a May morning or rimes a jingle for the nursery or puts together a couplet to give point to a fragment of proverbial wisdom, is nearly always exact in the repetition of his vowel. Where he is careless is in the accompanying consonants. As is remarked by the British critic from whom quotation has already been made, "we may observe that in all early European poetry, from the 'Song of Roland' to the popular ballads, the ear was satisfied with assonance, that is, the harmony of the vowel sounds; *hat* is assonant to *tag*, and that was good enough." So in the proverbial couplet,

> See a pin and pick it *up*,
> All day long you'll have good *luck*.

So again more than once in the unaffected lyrics of the laureate of the nursery, Mother Goose:

> Goosy, goosy *gander*,
>   Where do you *wander*?
> Upstairs and downstairs,
>   And in my lady's *chamber*.
>
>   Leave them *alone*
>   And they will come *home*.

This assonance is visible in the linking of *wild wood* and *childhood*, which many versifiers have proffered as tho it was a double rime; it is to be seen again in Whittier's *main land* and *trainband*; and it is obvious in Mr. Bret Harte's 'Her Letter':

> Of that ride—that to me was the *rarest*;
>   Of—the something you said at the gate.
> Ah! Joe, then I wasn't an *heiress*
>   To the best-paying lead in the State.

Altho this substitution of assonance for rime is uncommon in the more literary lyrics, which we may suppose to have been composed with the pen, it is still frequently to be found in the popular song, born on the lips of the singer, and set down in black and white only as an afterthought. It abounds in the college songs which have been sung into being, and in the brisk ballads of the variety-show—which Planché neatly characterized as "most music-hall, most melancholy." In one dime song-book containing the words set to music by Mr. David Braham to enliven one of Mr. Edward Harrigan's amusing pictures of life among the lowly in the tenement-house districts of New York, there can be discovered at least a dozen instances of this use of assonance as tho it were rime:

> De gal's name is *Nannie*,
> And she's just left her *mammie*.

He can get a pair of crutches
  From the doctor, it's well *known*,
And feel like the King of Persia,
  When he goes marching *home*.

> One husband was a *toper*,
> The other was a *loafer*.

'T is there the solid *voters*
Wear Piccadilly *chokers*.

On Sundays, then, the *ladies*
With a hundred million *babies*.

To the poor of suffering Ireland:
  Time and time *again*;
We thank you for our countrymen,
  And Donavan is our *name*.

When these lines are sung, rough as they are, the ear is satisfied by the absolute identity of the final vowel, upon which the voice lingers—while the final consonant is elided or almost suppressed. It may be doubted whether one in a hundred of those who heard these songs ever discovered any deficiency in the rimes. In more literary ballads only an exact rime attains to the sterling standard; but in folk-songs, ancient and modern, assonance seems to be legal tender by tacit convention. When Benedick was trying to make a copy of verses for Beatrice, he declared that he could "find out no rime to *lady* but *baby*, an innocent rime"—a remark which shows us that Benedick's theory of riming was much the same as Mr. Harrigan's.

Probably, however, the attempt to substitute assonance for rime would be resented by many of the readers who are tolerant toward such departures from exactness as *heaven* and *shriven* or *grove* and *dove*. That is to say, the unliterary ear insists on the identity of the vowel while careless as to the consonant, and the literary ear insists on the identity of the consonant while not quite so careful as to the vowel. And here is another reason for exact accuracy, which satisfies alike the learned and the unlearned, and is also in accord with Herbert Spencer's principle. It is true, probably, that such minor divergencies as the mating of *home* and *alone* and of *shadow* and *meadow*—to take one of each class—are not generally conscious on the part of the poet himself. Nor are they generally noticed by the reader or the auditor; and even when noticed they are not always resented as offensive. But just so long as there is a chance that they may be noticed and that they may be resented, they had best be avoided. The poet avails himself of his license at his peril. That way danger lies.

It is in the 'Adventures of Philip' that Thackeray records his hero's disapproval of a poet who makes *fire* rime with *Marire*. Even if the rime is made accurate to the ear, it is only by convicting the lyrist of carelessness of speech—not to call it vulgarity of pronunciation. But Dr. Holmes himself, sharp as he was upon those who rimed *dawn* and *morn*, was none the less guilty of a peccadillo quite as reprehensible—*Elizas* and *advertisers*. Whittier ventured to chain *Eva* not only with *leave her* and *receive her*, which suggest a slovenly utterance, but also with *give her*, *river*, and *never*, which are all of them wrenched from their true sounds to force them unto a vain and empty semblance of a rime. A kindred cockney recklessness can be found in one of Mrs. Browning's misguided modernizations of Chaucer:

> Now grant my ship some smooth haven *win her*;
> I follow Statius first, and then *Corinna*.

In each of these cases the poet takes out a wedding license for his couplet, only at the cost of compelling the reader to miscall the names of these ladies, and to address them as *Marire, Elizer, Ever*, and *Corinner*; and tho the rimes themselves are thus placed beyond reproach, the poet is revealed as regardless of all delicacy and precision of speech. Surely such a vulgarity of pronunciation is as disenchanting as any vulgarity in grammar.

Not quite so broad in the mispronunciation that makes these rimes are certain of Mr. Kipling's, as to which we are a little in doubt whether he is making his rime by violence to the normal sound or whether his own pronunciation is so abnormal that the rime itself seems to him accurate:

> Railways and roads they *wrought*
>   For the needs of the soil within;
> A time to scribble in *court*,
>   A time to bear and grin.

Long he pondered o'er the question in his scantly furnished *quarters*,
Then proposed to Minnie Boffkin, eldest of Judge Boffkin's *daughters*.

> I quarrel with my wife at home.
>   We never fight *abroad*;
> But Mrs. B. has grasped the fact,
>   I am her only *lord*.

Far less offensive than this wilful slovenliness, and yet akin to it, is the trick of forcing an emphasis upon a final syllable which is naturally short, in order that it may be made to rime with a syllable which is naturally long. For example, in the exquisite lyric of Lovelace's, 'To Althea from Prison,' in the second quatrain of the second stanza we find that we must prolong the final syllable of the final word:

> When thirsty grief in wine we steep,
>   When healths and draughts go *free*,
> Fishes that tipple in the deep
>   Know no such liber*ty*.

Here the rime evades us unless we read the last word *libertee*. But what then are we to do with the same word in the second quatrain of the first stanza? To get his rime here, the poet insists on our reading the last word *libertie*:

> When I lie tangled in her hair
>   And fettered to her *eye*,
> The birds that wanton in the air
>   Know no such liber*ty*.

Lovelace thus forces us not only to give an arbitrary pronunciation to the final word of his refrain, but also to vary this arbitrary pronunciation from stanza to stanza, awkwardly arresting our attention to no purpose, when we ought to be yielding ourselves absolutely to the charm of his most charming poem. Many another instance of this defect in craftsmanship can be discovered in the English poets, one of them in a lyric by that master of metrics, Poe, who opens the 'Haunted Palace' with a quatrain in which *tenanted* is made to mate with *head*:

> In the greenest of our valleys,
>   By good angels tenan*ted*,
> Once a fair and stately palace—
>   Radiant palace—reared its *head*.

In the one poem of Walt Whitman's in which he seemed almost willing to submit to the bonds of rime and meter, and which—perhaps for that reason partly—is the lyric of his now best known and best beloved, in 'O Captain, My Captain,' certain of the rimes are possible only by putting an impossible stress upon the final syllables of both words of the pair:

> The port is near, the bells I hear, the people all *exulting*,
> While follow eyes the steady keel, the vessel grim and *daring*.

And again:

> For you bouquets and ribbon'd wreaths, for you the shores *a-crowding*;
> For you they call, the swaying mass, their eager faces *turning*.

In all these cases—Lovelace's, Poe's, Whitman's—we find that the principle of Economy of Attention has been violated, with a resulting shock which diminishes somewhat our pleasure in the poems, delightful as they are, each in its several way. We have been called to bestow a momentary consideration on the mechanism of the poem, when we should have preferred to reserve all our power to receive the beauty of its spirit.

It may be doubted whether any pronunciation, however violently dislocated, can justify Whittier's joining of *bruised* and *crusade* in his 'To England,' or Browning's conjunction of *windows* and *Hindus* in his 'Youth and Art.' In 'Cristina' Browning tries to combine *moments* and *endowments*; in his 'Another Way of Love' he conjoins *spider* and *consider*; and in his 'Soliloquy in a Spanish Cloister' he binds together *horse-hairs* and *corsair's*. Perhaps one reason why Browning has made his way so slowly with the broad public—whom every poet must conquer at last, or in the end confess defeat—is that his rimes are sometimes violent and awkward, and sometimes complicated and arbitrary. The poet has reveled in his own ingenuity in compounding them, and so he flourishes them in the face of the reader. The principle of Economy of Attention demands that in serious verse the rime must be not only so accurate as to escape remark, but also wholly unstrained. It must seem natural, necessary, obvious, even inevitable, or else our minds are wrested from a rapt contemplation of the theme to a disillusioning consideration of the sounds by which it is bodied forth.

"Really the meter of some of the modern poems I have read," said Coleridge, "bears about the same relation to meter, properly understood, that dumb-bells do to music; both are for exercise, and pretty severe too, I think." A master of meter Browning proved himself again and again, very inventive in the new rhythms he introduced, and almost unfailingly felicitous; and yet there are poems of his in which the rimes impose on the reader a steady muscular exercise. In the 'Glove,' for example, there not only abound manufactured rimes, each of which in turn arrests the attention, and each of which demands a most conscientious articulation before the ear can apprehend it, but with a persistent perversity the poet puts the abnormal combination first, and puts last the normal word with which it is to be united in wedlock. Thus *aghast I'm* precedes *pastime*, and *well swear* comes before *elsewhere*. This is like presenting us with the answer before propounding the riddle.

In comic verse, of course, difficulty gaily vanquished may be a part of the joke, and an adroit and unexpected rime may be a witticism in itself. But in the 'Ingoldsby Legends' and in the 'Fable for Critics' it is generally the common word that comes before the uncommon combination the alert rimester devises to accompany it. When a line of Barham's ends with

Mephistopheles we wonder how he is going to solve the difficulty, and our expectation is swiftly gratified with *coffee lees*; and when Lowell informs us that Poe

... talks like a book of iambs and *pentameters*,

we bristle our ears while he adds:

In a way to make people of common sense *damn meters*.

But the 'Glove' is not comic in intent; the core of it is tragic, and the shell is at least romantic. Perhaps a hard and brilliant playfulness of treatment might not be out of keeping with the psychologic subtlety of its catastrophe; but not a few readers resentfully reject the misplaced ingenuity of the wilfully artificial double rimes. The incongruity between the matter of the poem and the manner of it attracts attention to the form, and leaves us the less for the fact.

It would be interesting to know just why Browning chose to do what he did in the 'Glove' and in more than one other poem. He had his reasons, doubtless, for he was no unconscious warbler of unpremeditated lays. If he refused to be loyal to the principle of Economy of Attention, he knew what he was doing. It was not from any heedlessness—like that of Emerson when he recklessly rimed *woodpecker* with *bear*; or like that of Lowell when he boldly insisted on riming the same *woodpecker* with *hear*. Emerson and Lowell—and Whittier also—it may be noted, were none of them enamoured of technic; and when a couplet or a quatrain or a stanza of theirs happened to attain perfection, as not infrequently they do, we cannot but feel it to be only a fortunate accident. They were not untiring students of versification, forever seeking to spy out its mysteries and to master its secrets, as Milton was, and Tennyson and Poe.

And yet no critic has more satisfactorily explained the essential necessity of avoiding discords than did Lowell when he affirmed that "not only meter but even rime itself is not without suggestion in outward nature. Look at the pine, how its branches, balancing each other, ray out from the tapering stem in stanza after stanza, how spray answers to spray, strophe and antistrophe, till the perfect tree stands an embodied ode, Nature's triumphant vindication of proportion, number, and harmony. Who can doubt the innate charm of rime who has seen the blue river repeat the blue o'erhead; who has been ravished by the visible consonance of the tree growing at once toward an upward and a downward heaven on the edge of the twilight cove; or who has watched how, as the kingfisher flitted from shore to shore, his visible echo flies under him, and completes the fleeting couplet in the visionary vault below?... You must not only expect, but you must expect in the right way; you must be magnetized beforehand in every fiber by your own sensibility in order that you may feel what and how you ought."

Here Lowell is in full agreement with Poe, who declared that "what, in rime, first and principally pleases, may be referred to the human sense or appreciation of equality." But there is no equality in the sound of *valleys* and *palace,* and so the human sense is robbed of its pleasure; and there is no consonance, visible or audible, between *woodpecker* and *hear,* and so we are suddenly demagnetized by our own sensibility, and cannot feel what and how we ought.

So long as the poet gives us rimes exact to the ear and completely satisfactory to the sense to which they appeal, he has solid ground beneath his feet; but if once he leaves this, then is chaos come again. Admit *given* and *heaven,* and it is hard to deny *chamber* and *remember.* Having relinquished the principle of uniformity of sound, you land yourself logically in the wildest anarchy. Allow *shadow* and *meadow* to be legitimate, and how can you put the bar sinister on *hear* and *woodpecker*? Indeed, we fail to see how you can help feeling that John Phœnix was unduly harsh when he rejected the poem of a Young Astronomer beginning, "O would I had a telescope with fourteen slides!" on account of the atrocious attempt in the second line to rime *Pleiades* with *slides*.

Lieutenant Derby was a humorist; but is his tying together of incompatible vocables much worse than one offense of which Keats is guilty?

> Then who would go
> Into dark Soho,
> And chatter with dack'd-haired *critics,*
> When he can stay
> For the new-mown hay
> And startle the dappled *prickets*?

This quotation is due to Professor F. N. Scott, who has drawn attention also to an astounding quatrain of Tennyson's 'Palace of Art':

> Or in a clear-wall'd city on the sea,
>   Near gilded organ-pipes, her *hair*
> Wound with white roses, slept St. Cecily;
>   An angel look'd at *her*.

Professor Scott declares that he hesitates "for a term by which to characterize such rimes as these. Certainly they are not eye-rimes in the proper meaning of that term. Perhaps ... they may be called nose-rimes."

Just as every instance of bad grammar interferes with the force of prose, so in verse every needless inversion and every defective rime interrupts the impression which the poet wishes to produce. There are really not so many in Pope's poems as there may seem to be, for since Queen Anne's day our language has modified its pronunciation here and there, leaving now only to the Irish the *tea* which is a perfect rime to *obey*, and the *join* which is a perfect rime to *line*.

Perhaps the prevalence in English verse of the intolerable "allowable rimes" is due in part to an acceptance of what seems like an evil precedent, to be explained away by our constantly changing pronunciation. Perhaps it is due in part also to the present wretched orthography of our language. The absurd "rimes to the eye" which abound in English are absent from Italian verse and from French. The French, as the inheritors through the Latin of the great Greek tradition, have a finer respect for form, and strive constantly for perfection of technic, altho the genius of their language seems to us far less lyric than ours. Théodore de Banville, in his little book on French versification, declared formally and emphatically that there is no such thing as a poetic license. And Voltaire, in a passage admirably rendered into English by the late Frederick Locker-Lampson, says that the French "insist that the rime shall cost nothing to the ideas, that it shall be neither trivial, nor too far-fetched; we exact vigorously in a verse the same purity, the same precision, as in prose. We do not admit the smallest license; we require an author to carry without a break all these chains, yet that he should appear ever free."

In a language as unrhythmic as the French, rime is far more important than it need be in a lilting and musical tongue like our own; but in the masterpieces of the English lyrists, as in those of the French, rime plays along the edges of a poem, ever creating the expectation it swiftly satisfies and giving most pleasure when its presence is felt and not flaunted. Like the dress of the well-bred woman, which sets off her beauty without attracting attention to itself, rime must be adequate and unobtrusive, neither too fine nor too shabby, but always in perfect taste.

(1898-1900)

XI
ON THE POETRY OF PLACE-NAMES

Plutarch tells us that the tragedian Æsopus, when he spoke the opening lines of the 'Atreus,' a tragedy by Attius,

> I'm Lord of Argos, heir of Pelops' crown.
> As far as Helle's sea and Ion's main
> Beat on the Isthmus,

entered so keenly into the spirit of this lofty passage that he struck dead at his feet a slave who approached too near to the person of royalty; and Professor Tyrrel notes how these verses affect us with "the weight of names great in myth-land and hero-land," and he suggests that they produce "a vague impression of majesty," like Milton's

> Jousted in Aspromont or Montalban,
> Damasco or Morocco or Trebizond,
> Or whom Biserta sent from Afric's shore,
> When Charlemagne with all his peerage fell
> By Fontarabia.

It is a question how far the beauty of the resonant lines of the 'Agamemnon' of Æschylus, where the news of the fall of Troy is flashed along the chain of beacons from hilltop to promontory, is due even more to the mere sounds of the proper names than it is to the memories these mighty names evoke. Far inferior to this, and yet deriving its effect also from the sonorous roll of the lordly proper names (which had perhaps lingered in the poet's memory ever since the travels of his childhood), is the passage in the 'Hernani' of Victor Hugo, when, the new emperor ordering all the conspirators to be set free who are not of noble blood, the hero steps forward hotly to declare his rank:

> Puisqu'il faut être grand pour mourir, je me lève.
> Dieu qui donne le sceptre et qui te le donna
> M'a fait duc de Segorbe et duc de Cardona,
> Marquis de Mouroy, comte Albatera, vicomte

> De Gor, seigneur de lieux dont j'ignore le compte.
> Je suis Jean d'Aragon, grand maître d'Avis, né
> Dans l'exil, fils proscrit d'un père assassiné
> Par sentence du tien, roi Carlos de Castille!

Lowell, after telling us that "precisely what makes the charm of poetry is what we cannot explain any more than we can describe a perfume," proceeds to point out that it is a prosaic passage of Drayton's 'Polyolbion' which gave a hint to Wordsworth, thus finely utilized in one of the later bard's 'Poems on the Naming of Places':

> Joanna, looking in my eyes, beheld
> That ravishment of mine, and laughed aloud.
> The Rock, like something starting from a sleep,
> Took up the Lady's voice, and laughed again;
> The ancient Woman seated on Helm-crag
> Was ready with her cavern; Hammar-scar,
> And the tall steep of Silver-how, sent forth
> A noise of laughter; southern Loughrigg heard,
> And Fairfield answered with a mountain tone;
> Helvellyn, far into the clear blue sky,
> Carried the Lady's voice,—old Skiddaw blew
> His speaking-trumpet;—back out of the clouds
> Of Glaramara southward came the voice;
> And Kirkstone tossed it from his misty head.

Not a little of this same magic is there in many a line of Walt Whitman; especially did he rejoice to point out the beauty of Manahatta:

> I was asking something specific and perfect for my city,
> Whereupon lo! upsprang the aboriginal name.

Longfellow has recorded his feeling that

> The destined walls
> Of Cambalu and of Cathain Can

(from the eleventh book of 'Paradise Lost') is a "delicious line." Longfellow was always singularly sensitive to the magic power of words, and not long after that entry in his journal there is this other: "I always write the name October with especial pleasure. There is a secret charm about it, not to be defined. It is full of memories, it is full of dusky splendors, it is full of glorious poetry." And Poe was so taken with the melody of this same word that in 'Ulalume' he invented a proper name merely that he might have a rime for it:

> It was night in the lonesome October
>   Of my most immemorial year;
> It was hard by the dim lake of Auber,
>   In the misty mid-region of Weir—
> It was down by the dank tarn of Auber,
>   In the ghoul-haunted woodland of Weir.

The charm of these lines is due mainly to their modulated music, and to the contrast of the vowel sounds in *Auber* and *Weir*, just as a great part of the beauty of Landor's exquisite lyric, 'Rose Aylmer,' is contained in the name itself. Is there any other reason why Mesopotamia should be a "blessed word," save that its vowels and its consonants are so combined as to fill the ear with sweetness? Yet Mr. Lecky records Garrick's assertion that Whitefield could pronounce Mesopotamia so as to make a congregation weep. And others have found delight in repeating a couplet of Campbell's:

> And heard across the waves' tumultuous roar
> The wolfs long howl from Oonalaska's shore—

a delight due, I think, chiefly to the unexpected combination of open vowels and sharp consonants in the single Eskimo word, the meaning of it being unknown and wholly unimportant, and the sound of it filling the ear with an uncertain and yet awaited pleasure.

Just as Oonalaska strikes us at once as the fit title for a shore along which the lone wolf should howl, so Atchafalaya bears in its monotonous vowel a burden of melancholy, made more pitiful to us by our knowledge that it was the name of the dark water where Evangeline and Gabriel almost met in the night and then parted again for years. Charles Sumner wrote to Longfellow that Mrs. Norton considered "the scene on the Lake Atchafalaya, where the two lovers pass each other, so typical of life that she had a seal cut with that name upon it"; and shortly afterward Leopold, the King of the Belgians, speaking of 'Evangeline,' "asked her if she did not think the word Atchafalaya was suggestive of experience in life, and added that he was about to have it cut on a seal"—whereupon, to his astonishment, she showed him hers.

It would be difficult indeed to declare how much of the delight our ear may take in these words—Atchafalaya, Oonalaska, Mesopotamia,—is due simply to their own melody, and how much to the memories they may stir. Here we may see one reason why the past seems so much more romantic than the present. In tales of olden time even the proper names linger in our ears with an echo of "the glory that was Greece and the grandeur that was Rome." Here is, in fact, an unfair advantage which dead-and-gone heroes of foreign birth have over the men of our own day and our own country. "If we dilate in beholding the Greek energy, the Roman pride, it is that we are already domesticating the same sentiment," said Emerson in his essay on 'Heroism,' and he added that the first step of our worthiness was "to disabuse us of our superstitious associations with places and times." And he asks, "Why should these words, Athenian, Roman, Asia, and England, so tingle in the ear? Where the heart is, there the muses, there the gods sojourn, and not in any geography of fame. Massachusetts, Connecticut River, and Boston Bay you think paltry places, and the ear loves the names of foreign and classic topography. But here we are; and if we hurry a little, we may come to learn that here is best.... The Jerseys were honest ground enough for Washington to tread."

Emerson penned these sentences in the first half of the nineteenth century, when we Americans were still fettered by the inherited shackles of colonialism. Fifty years after he wrote, it would have been hard to find an American who thought either Boston Bay or Massachusetts a paltry place. And Matthew Arnold has recorded that to him, when he was an undergraduate, Emerson was then "but a voice speaking from three thousand miles away; but so well he spoke that from that time forth Boston Bay and Concord were names invested to my ear with a sentiment akin to that which invests for me the names of Oxford and Weimar."

As for the Connecticut River, had not Thoreau done it the service Irving had rendered long before to the Hudson?—had he not given it a right to be set down in the geography of literature? It is well that we should be reminded now and again that the map which the lover of letters has in his mind's eye is different by a whole world from the projection which the school-boy smears with his searching finger, since the tiny little rivers on whose banks great men grew to maturity, the Tiber and the Po, the Seine and the Thames, flow across its pages with a fuller stream than any Kongo or Amazon. And on this literary map the names of not a few American rivers and hills and towns are now inscribed.

It is fortunate that many of the American places most likely to be mentioned in the poetic gazetteer have kept the liquid titles the aborigines gave them. "I climbed one of my hills yesterday afternoon and took a sip of Wachusett, who was well content that Monadnock was out of the way," wrote Lowell in a letter. "How lucky our mountains (many of them) are in their names, tho they must find it hard to live up to them sometimes! The Anglo-Saxon sponsor would Nicodemus 'em to nothing in no time." It will be pitiful if the Anglo-Saxons on the Pacific coast allow Mount Tacoma to be Nicodemused to Mount Rainier, as the Anglo-Saxons of the Atlantic coast allowed Lake Andiatarocte to be Nicodemused into Lake George. Fenimore Cooper strove in vain for the acceptance of Horicon as the name of this lovely sheet of water, which the French discoverer called the Lake of the Holy Sacrament.

Marquette spoke of a certain stream as the River of the Immaculate Conception, altho the Spaniards were already familiar with it as the River of the Holy Spirit; and later La Salle called it after Colbert; but an Algonquin word meaning "many waters" clung to it always; and so we know it now as the Mississippi. The Spaniard has been gone from its banks for more than a hundred years, and the Frenchman has followed the Indian, and the Anglo-Saxon now holds the mighty river from its source to its many mouths; but the broad stream bears to-day the name the red men gave it. And so also the Ohio keeps its native name, tho the French hesitated between St. Louis and La Belle Rivière as proper titles for it. Cataraqui is one old name for an American river, and Jacques Cartier accepted for this stream another Indian word, Hochelaga, but (as Professor Hinsdale reminded us) "St. Lawrence, the name that Cartier had given to the Gulf, unfortunately superseded it."

Much of the charm of these Indian words, Atchafalaya, Ohio, Andiatarocte, Tacoma, is due no doubt to their open vowels; but is not some of it to be ascribed to our ignorance of their meanings? We may chance to know that Mississippi signifies "many waters" and that Minnehaha can be interpreted as "laughing water," but that is the furthermost border of our knowledge. If we were all familiar with the Algonquin dialects, I fancy that the fascination of many of these names would fade swiftly. And yet perhaps it would not, for we could never be on as friendly terms with the Indian language as we are with our own; and there is ever a suggestion of the mystic in the foreign tongue.

We engrave *Souvenir* on our sweetheart's bracelet or brooch; but the French for this purpose prefer *Remember*. "The difficulty of translation lies in the *color* of words," Longfellow declared. "Is the Italian *ruscilletto gorgoglioso* fully rendered by *gurgling brooklet*? Or the Spanish *pojaros vocingleros* by *garrulous birds*? Something seems wanting. Perhaps it is only the fascination of foreign and unfamiliar sounds; and to the Italian and Spanish ear the English words may seem equally beautiful."

After the death of the Duke of Wellington, Longfellow wrote a poem on the 'Warden of the Cinque Ports'; and to us Americans there was poetry in the very title. And yet it may be questioned whether the Five Ports are necessarily any more poetic than the Five Points or the Seven Dials. So also Sanguelac strikes us as far loftier than Bloody Pond, but is it really? I have wondered often whether to a Jew of the first century Aceldama, the field of blood, and Golgotha, the place of a skull, were not perfectly commonplace designations, quite as common, in fact, as Bone Gulch or Hangman's Hollow would be to us, and conveying the same kind of suggestion.

We are always prone to accept the unknown as the magnificent,—if I may translate the Latin phrase,—to put a higher value on the things veiled from us by the folds of a foreign language. The Bosporus is a more poetic place than Oxford, tho the meaning of both names is the same. Montenegro fills our ears and raises our expectations higher than could any mere Black Mountain. The "Big River" is but a vulgar nickname, and yet we accept the equivalent Guadalquivir and Rio Grande; we even allow ourselves sometimes to speak of the Rio Grande River—which is as tautological as De Quincey declared the name of Mrs. Barbauld to be. Bridgeport is as prosaic as may be, while Alcantara has a remote and romantic aroma, and yet the latter word signifies only "the bridge." We can be neighborly, most of us, with the White Mountains; but we feel a deeper respect for Mont Blanc and the Weisshorn and the Sierra Nevada.

Sometimes the hard facts are twisted arbitrarily to force them into an imported falsehood. Elberon, where Garfield died, was founded by one L.

B. Brown, so they say, and the homely name of the owner was thus contorted to make a seemingly exotic appellation for the place. And they say also that the man who once dammed a brook amid the pines of New Jersey had three children, Carrie, Sally, and Joe, and that he bestowed their united names upon Lake Carasaljo, the artificial piece of water on the banks of which Lakewood now sits salubriously. In Mr. Cable's 'John March, Southerner,' one of the characters explains: "You know an ancestor of his founded Suez. That's how it got its name. His name was Ezra and hers was Susan, don't you see?" And I have been told of a town on the Northern Pacific Railroad which the first comers called Hell-to-Pay, and which has since experienced a change of heart and become Eltopia.

In the third quarter of the nineteenth century a thirst for self-improvement raged among the villages of the lower Hudson River, and many a modest settlement thought to better itself and to rise in the world by the assumption of a more swelling style and title. When a proposition was made to give up the homely Dobbs Ferry for something less plebeian, the poet of 'Nothing to Wear' rimed a pungent protest:

> They say "Dobbs" ain't melodious;
> It's "horrid," "vulgar," "odious";
>   In all their crops it sticks;
> And then the worse addendum
> Of "Ferry" does offend 'em
>   More than its vile prefix.
> Well, it does seem distressing,
> But, if I'm good at guessing,
>   Each one of these same nobs
> If there was money in it,
> Would ferry in a minute,
>   And change his name to Dobbs!
>
> That's it—they're not partic'lar
> Respecting the auric'lar
>   At a stiff market rate;
> But Dobbs's special vice is
> That he keeps down the prices
>   Of all their real estate!

> A name so unattractive
> Keeps villa-sites inactive,
>   And spoils the broker's jobs;
> They think that speculation
> Would rage at "Paulding's Station,"
>   Which stagnates now at "Dobbs."

In the later stanzas Mr. Butler denounces changes nearer to New York:

> Down there, on old Manhattan,
> Where land-sharks breed and fatten,
>   They wiped out Tubby Hook.
> That famous promontory,
> Renowned in song and story,
>   Which time nor tempest shook,
> Whose name for aye had been good,
> Stands newly christened "Inwood,"
>   And branded with the shame
> Of some old rogue who passes
> By dint of aliases,
>   Afraid of his own name!
>
> See how they quite outrival
> Plain barn-yard Spuyten Duyvil
>   By peacock Riverdale,
> Which thinks all else it conquers,
> And over homespun Yonkers
>   Spreads out its flaunting tail!

No loyal Manhattaner but would regret to part with Spuyten Duyvil and Yonkers and Harlem, and the other good old names that recall the good old Dutchmen who founded New Amsterdam. Few loyal Manhattaners, I think, but would be glad to see the Greater New York (now at last an accomplished fact) dignified by a name less absurd than New York. If Pesth and Buda could come together and become Budapest, why may not the Greater New York resume the earlier name and be known to the world as Manhattan? Why should the people of this great city of ours let the Anglo-Saxons "Nicodemus us to nothing," or less than nothing, with a name so pitiful as New York? "I hope and trust," wrote Washington Irving, "that we are to live to be an old nation, as well as our neighbors, and have no idea that our cities when they shall have attained to venerable antiquity shall still be dubbed New York and New London and new this and new that, like the Pont Neuf (the new bridge) at Paris, which is the oldest bridge in that capital, or like the Vicar of Wakefield's horse, which continued to be called the colt until he died of old age."

Whenever any change shall be made we must hope that the new will be not only more euphonious than the old, but more appropriate and more stately. Perhaps Hangtown in California made a change for the better many years ago when it took the name of Placerville; but perhaps Placerville was not the best name it could have taken. "We will be nothing but Anglo-Saxons in the old world or in the new," wrote Matthew Arnold when he was declaring the beauty of Celtic literature; "and when our race has built Bold Street in Liverpool, and pronounced it very good, it hurries across the Atlantic, and builds Nashville and Jacksonville and Milledgeville, and thinks it is fulfilling the designs of Providence in an incomparable manner." In this sentence the criticism cuts both British habits and American. Later in life Matthew Arnold sharpened his knife again for use on the United States alone. "What people," he asked, "in whom the sense for beauty and fitness was quick, could have invented or tolerated the hideous names ending in *ville*—the Briggsvilles, Higginsvilles, Jacksonvilles—rife from Maine to Florida?"

Now, it must be confessed at once that we have no guard against a thrust like that. Such names do abound and they are of unsurpassed hideousness. But could not the same blow have got home as fatally had it been directed against his own country? A glance at any gazetteer of the British Isles would show that the British are quite as vulnerable as the Americans. In fact, this very question of Matthew Arnold's suggested to an anonymous American rimester the perpetration of a copy of verses, the quality of which can be gaged by these first three stanzas:

> Of Briggsville and Jacksonville
>   I care not now to sing;
> They make me sad and very mad—
>   My inmost soul they wring.
> I'll hie me back to England,
>   And straightway I will go

To Boxford and to Swaffham,
   To Plunger and Loose Hoe.

At Scrooby and at Gonerby,
   At Wigton and at Smeeth,
At Bottesford and Runcorn,
   I need not grit my teeth.
At Swineshead and at Crummock,
   At Sibsey and Spithead,
Stoke Poges and Wolsoken
   I will not wish me dead.

At Horbling and at Skidby,
   At Chipping Ongar, too,
At Botterel Stotterdon and Swops,
   At Skellington and Skew,
At Piddletown and Blumsdown,
   At Shanklin and at Smart,
At Gosberton and Wrangle
   I'll soothe this aching heart.

To discover a mote in our neighbor's eyes does not remove the mote in our own, however much immediate relief it may give us from the acuteness of our pain. When Matthew Arnold animadverted upon "the jumbles of unnatural and inappropriate names everywhere," he may have had in mind the most absurd medley existing anywhere in the world—the handful of Greek and Roman names of all sorts which was sown broadcast over the western part of New York State. Probably this region of misfortune it was that Irving was thinking about when he denounced the "shallow affectation of scholarship," and told how "the whole catalog of ancient worthies is shaken out of the back of Lemprière's Classical Dictionary, and a wide region of wild country is sprinkled over with the names of heroes, poets, sages of antiquity, jumbled into the most whimsical juxtaposition."

Along the road from Dublin, going south to Bray, the traveler finds Dumdrum and Stillorgan, as tho—to quote the remarks of the Irish friend who gave me these facts—a band of wandering musicians had broken up and scattered their names along the highway. For sheer ugliness it would be hard to beat two other proper names near Dublin, where the Sallynoggin road runs into the Glenageary.

It may be that these words sound harsher in our strange ears than they do to a native wonted to their use. We take the unknown for the magnificent sometimes, no doubt; but sometimes also we take it for the ridiculous. To us New-Yorkers, for instance, there is nothing absurd or ludicrous in the sturdy name of Schenectady; perhaps there is even a hint of stateliness in the syllables. But when Mr. Laurence Hutton was in the north of Scotland some years ago there happened to be in his party a young lady from that old Dutch town; and when a certain laird who lived in those parts chanced to be told that this young lady dwelt in Schenectady he was moved to inextinguishable laughter. He ejaculated the outlandish sounds again and again in the sparse intervals of his boisterous merriment. He announced to all his neighbors that among their visitors was a young lady from Schenectady, and all who called were presented to her, and at every repetition of the strange syllables his violent cachinnations broke forth afresh. Never had so comic a name fallen upon his ears; and yet he himself was the laird of Balduthro (pronounced Balduthy); his parish was Ironcross (pronounced Aron-crouch); his railway-station was Kilconquhar (pronounced Kinŏcher); and his post-office was Pittenweem!

Robert Louis Stevenson was a Scotchman who had changed his point of view more often than the laird of Balduthro; he had a broader vision and a more delicate ear and a more refined perception of humor. When he came to these United States as an amateur immigrant on his way across the plains, he asked the name of a river from a brakeman on the train; and when he heard that the stream "was called the Susquehanna, the beauty of the name seemed part and parcel of the beauty of the land. As when Adam with divine fitness named the creatures, so this word Susquehanna was at once accepted by the fancy. That was the name, as no other could be, for that shining river and desirable valley."

And then Stevenson breaks from his narrative to sing the praises of our place-names. The passage is long for quotation in a paper where too much has been quoted already; and yet I should be derelict to my duty if I did not transcribe it here. Stevenson had lived among many peoples, and he was far more cosmopolitan than Matthew Arnold, and more willing, therefore, to dwell on beauties than on blemishes. "None can care for literature in itself," he begins, "who do not take a special pleasure in the sound of names; and there is no part of the world where nomenclature is so rich, poetical, humorous, and picturesque as the United States of America. All times, races, and languages have brought their contribution. Pekin is in the same State with Euclid, with Bellefontaine, and with Sandusky. Chelsea, with its London associations of red brick, Sloane Square, and the King's Road, is own suburb to stately and primeval Memphis; there they have their seat, translated names of cities, where the Mississippi runs by Tennessee and Arkansas.... Old, red Manhattan lies, like an Indian arrow-head under a steam-factory, below Anglified New York. The names of the States and Territories themselves form a chorus of sweet and most romantic vocables: Delaware, Ohio, Indiana, Florida, Dakota, Iowa, Wyoming, Minnesota, and the Carolinas; there are few poems with a nobler music for the ear; a songful, tuneful land; and if the new Homer shall arise from the western continent, his verse will be enriched, his pages sing spontaneously, with the names of states and cities that would strike the fancy in a business circular."

As Campbell had utilized the innate beauty of the word Wyoming, so Stevenson himself made a ballad on the dreaded name of Ticonderoga; and these are two of the proper names of modern America that sing themselves. But there is nothing canorous in Anglified New York; there is no sonority in its syllables; there is neither dignity nor truth in its obvious meaning. It might serve well enough as the address of a steam-factory in a business circular; but it lacks absolutely all that the name of a metropolis demands. Stevenson thought that the new Homer would joy in working into his strong lines the beautiful nomenclature of America; but Washington Irving had the same anticipation, and it forced him to declare that if New York "were to share the fate of Troy itself, to suffer a ten years' siege, and be sacked and plundered, no modern Homer would ever be able to elevate the name to epic dignity." Irving went so far as to wish not only that New York city should be Manhattan again, but that New York State should be Ontario, the Hudson River the Mohegan, and the United States themselves Appalachia. Edgar Allan Poe, than whom none of our poets had a keener perception of the beauty of sounds and the fitness of words, approved of Appalachia as the name of the whole country.

Perhaps we must wait yet a little while for Appalachia and Ontario and the Mohegan; but has not the time come to dig up that old red arrow-head

XII
AS TO "AMERICAN SPELLING"

[This paper is here reprinted from an earlier volume now out of print.]

When the author of the 'Cathedral' was accosted by the wandering Englishmen within the lofty aisles of Chartres, he cracked a joke,

> Whereat they stared, then laughed, and we were friends.
> The seas, the wars, the centuries interposed,
> Abolished in the truce of common speech
> And mutual comfort of the mother-tongue.

In this common speech other Englishmen are not always ready to acknowledge the full rights of Lowell's countrymen. They would put us off with but a younger brother's portion of the mother-tongue, seeming somehow to think that they are more closely related to the common parent than we are. But Orlando, the younger son of Sir Rowland du Bois, was no villain; and tho we have broken with the fatherland, the mother-tongue is none the less our heritage. Indeed, we need not care whether the division is *per stirpes* or *per capita*; our share is not the less in either case.

Beneath the impotent protests which certain British newspapers are prone to make every now and again against the "American language" as a whole, and against the stray Americanism which has happened last to invade England, there is a tacit assumption that we Americans are outer barbarians, mere strangers, wickedly tampering with something which belongs to the British exclusively. And the outcry against the "American language" is not as shrill nor as piteous as the shriek of horror with which certain of the journals of London greet "American spelling," a hideous monster which they feared was ready to devour them as soon as the international copyright bill should become law. In the midst of every discussion of the effect of the copyright act in Great Britain, the bugbear of "American spelling" reared its grisly head. The London *Times* declared that English publishers would never put any books into type in the United States because the people of England would never tolerate the peculiarities of orthography which prevailed in American printing-offices. The *St. James's Gazette* promptly retorted that "already newspapers in London are habitually using the ugliest forms of American spelling, and these silly eccentricities do not make the slightest difference in their circulation." The *Times* and the *St. James's Gazette* might differ as to the effect of the copyright act on the profits of the printers of England, but they agreed heartily as to the total depravity of "American spelling." I think that any disinterested foreigner who might chance to hear these violent outcries would suppose that English orthography was as the law of the Medes and Persians, which altereth not; he would be justified in believing that the system of spelling now in use in Great Britain was hallowed by the Established Church, and in some way mysteriously connected with the state religion.

Just what the British newspapers were afraid of it is not easy to say, and it is difficult to declare just what they mean when they talk of "American spelling." Probably they do not refer to the improvements in orthography suggested by the first great American—Benjamin Franklin. Possibly they do refer to the modifications in the accepted spelling proposed by another American, Noah Webster—not so great, and yet not to be named slightingly by any one who knows how fertile his labors have been for the good of the whole country. Noah Webster, so his biographer, Mr. Scudder, tells us, "was one of the first to carry a spirit of democracy into letters.... Throughout his work one may detect a confidence in the common sense of the people which was as firm as Franklin's." But the innovations of Webster were hesitating and often inconsistent; and most of them have been abandoned by later editors of Webster's American Dictionary of the English Language.

What, then, do British writers mean when they animadvert upon "American spelling"? So far as I have been able to discover, the British journalists object to certain minor labor-saving improvements of American orthography, such as the dropping of the *k* from *almanack*, the omission of one *g* from *waggon*, and the like; and they protest with double force, with all the strength that in them lies, against the substitution of a single *l* for a double *l* in such words as *traveller*, against the omission of the *u* from such words as *honour*, against the substitution of an *s* for a *c* in such words as *defence*, and against the transposing of the final two letters of such words as *theatre*. The objection to "American spelling" may lie deeper than I have here suggested, and it may have a wider application; but I have done my best to state it fully and fairly as I have deduced it from a painful perusal of many columns of exacerbated British writing.

Now if I have succeeded in stating honestly the extent of the British journalistic objections to "American spelling," the unprejudiced reader may be moved to ask: "Is this all? Are these few and slight and unimportant changes the cause of this mighty commotion?" One may agree with Sainte-Beuve in thinking that "orthography is the beginning of literature," without discovering in these modifications from the Johnsonian canon any cause for extreme disgust. And since I have quoted Sainte-Beuve once, I venture to cite him again, and to take from the same letter of March 15, 1867, his suggestion that "if we write more correctly, let it be to express especially honest feelings and just thoughts."

Feelings may be honest tho they are violent, but irritation is not the best frame of mind for just thinking. The tenacity with which some of the newspapers of London are wont to defend the accepted British orthography is perhaps due rather to feeling than to thought. Lowell told us that esthetic hatred burned nowadays with as fierce a flame as ever once theological hatred; and any American who chances to note the force and the fervor and the frequency of the objurgations against "American spelling" in the columns of the *Saturday Review*, for example, and of the *Athenæum*, may find himself wondering as to the date of the papal bull which declared the infallibility of contemporary British orthography, and as to the place where the council of the church was held at which it was made an article of faith.

The *Saturday Review* and the *Athenæum*, highly pitched as their voices are, yet are scarcely shriller in their cry to arms against the possible invasion of the sanctity of British orthography by "American spelling" than is the London *Times*, the solid representative of British thought, the mighty organ-voice of British feeling. Yet the *Times* is not without orthographic eccentricities of its own, as Matthew Arnold took occasion to point out. In his essay on the 'Literary Influence of Academies,' he asserted that "every one has noticed the way in which the *Times* chooses to spell the word *diocese*; it always spells it *diocess*, deriving it, I suppose, from *Zeus* and *census*.... Imagine an educated Frenchman indulging himself in an orthographical antic of this sort!"

When we read what is written in the *Times* and the *Saturday Review* and the *Athenæum*, sometimes in set articles on the subject, and even more often in casual and subsidiary slurs in the course of book-reviews, we wonder at the vehemence of the feeling displayed. If we did not know that ancient abuses are often defended with more violence and with louder shouts than inheritances of less doubtful worth, we might suppose that the present spelling of the English language was in a condition perfectly satisfactory alike to scholar and to student. Such, however, is not the case. The leading philologists of Great Britain and of the United States have repeatedly denounced English spelling as it now is on both sides of the Atlantic, Professor Max Müller at Oxford being no less emphatic than Professor Whitney at Yale. There is now living no scholar of any repute who any longer defends the ordinary orthography of the English language.

The fact is that a little learning is quite as dangerous a thing now as it was in Pope's day. Those who are volubly denouncing "American spelling" in the columns of British journals are not students of the history of English speech; they are not scholars in English; in so far as they know anything of the language, they are but amateur philologists. As a well-known writer on spelling reform once neatly remarked, "The men who get their etymology by inspiration are like the poor in that we have them always with us." Altho few of them are as ignorant and dense as the unknown unfortunate who first tortured the obviously jocular *Welsh rabbit* into a ridiculously impossible *Welsh rarebit*, still the most of their writing serves no good purpose. Nor do we discover in these specimens of British journalism that abundant urbanity which etymology might lead us to look for in the writing of inhabitants of so large a city as London.

Any one who takes the trouble to inform himself on the subject will soon discover that it is chiefly the half-educated men who defend the contemporary orthography of the English language, and who denounce the alleged "American spelling" of *center* and *honor*. The uneducated reader may wonder perchance what the *g* is doing in *sovereign*; the half-educated reader discerns in the *g* a connecting-link between the English *sovereign* and the Latin *regno*; the well-educated reader knows that there is no philological connection whatever between *regno* and *sovereign*.

Most of those who write with ease in British journals, deploring the prevalence of "American spelling," have never carried their education so far as to acquire that foundation of wisdom which prevents a man from expressing an opinion on subjects as to which he is ignorant. The object of education, it has been said, is to make a man know what he knows, and also to know how much he does not know. Despite the close sympathy between the intellectual pursuits, a student of optics is not necessarily qualified to express an opinion in esthetics; and on the other hand, a critic of art may easily be ignorant of science. Now literature is one of the arts, and philology is a science. Altho men of letters have to use words as the tools of their trade, orthography is none the less a branch of philology, and philology does not come by nature. Literature may even exist without writing, and therefore without spelling. Writing, indeed, has no necessary connection with literature; still less has orthography. A literary critic is rarely a scientific student of language; he has no need to be; but being ignorant, it is the part of modesty for him not to expose his ignorance. To boast of it is unseemly.

Far be it from me to appear as the defender of the "American spelling" which the British journalists denounce. This "American spelling" is less absurd than the British spelling only in so far as it has varied therefrom. Even in these variations there is abundant absurdity. Once upon a time most words that now are spelled with a final *c* had an added *k*. Even now both British and American usage retains this *k* in *hammock*, altho both British and Americans have dropped the needless letter from *havoc*; while the British retain the *k* at the end of *almanack* and the Americans have dropped it. Dr. Johnson was a reactionary in orthography as in politics; and in his dictionary he wilfully put a final *k* to words like *optick*, without being generally followed by the publick—as he would have spelled it. *Music* was then *musick*, altho, even as late as Aubrey's time, it had been *musique*. In our own day we are witnessing the very gradual substitution of the logical *technic* for the form originally imported from France—*technique*.

I am inclined to think that *technic* is replacing *technique* more rapidly—or should I say less slowly?—in the United States than in Great Britain. We Americans like to assimilate our words and to make them our own, while the British have rather a fondness for foreign phrases. A London journalist recently held up to public obloquy as an "ignorant Americanism" the word *program,* altho he would have found it set down in Professor Skeat's Etymological Dictionary. "*Programme* was taken from the French," so a recent writer reminds us, "and in violation of analogy, seeing that, when it was imported into English, we had already *anagram, cryptogram, diagram, epigram,* etc." The logical form *program* is not common even in America; and British writers seem to prefer the French form, as British speakers still give a French pronunciation to *charade,* and to *trait,* which in America have long since been accepted frankly as English words.

Possibly it is idle to look for any logic in anything which has to do with modern English orthography on either side of the ocean. Perhaps, however, there is less even than ordinary logic in the British journalist's objection to the so-called "American spelling" of *meter;* for why should any one insist on *metre* while unhesitatingly accepting its compound *diameter*? Mr. John Bellows, in the preface to his inestimable French-English and English-French pocket dictionary, one of the very best books of reference ever published, informs us that "the act of Parliament legalizing the use of the metric system in this country [England] gives the words *meter, liter, gram,* etc., spelled on the American plan." Perhaps now that the sanction of law has been given to this spelling, the final *er* will drive out the *re* which has usurped its place. In one of the last papers that he wrote, Lowell declared that "*center* is no Americanism; it entered the language in that shape, and kept it at least as late as Defoe." "In the sixteenth and in the first half of the seventeenth century," says Professor Lounsbury, "while both ways of writing these words existed side by side, the termination *er* is far more common than that in *re*. The first complete edition of Shakspere's plays was published in 1623. In that work *sepulcher* occurs thirteen times; it is spelled eleven times with *er*. *Scepter* occurs thirty-seven times; it is not once spelled with *re,* but always with *er*. *Center* occurs twelve times, and in nine instances out of the twelve it ends in *er*." So we see that this so-called "American spelling" is fully warranted by the history of the English language. It is amusing to note how often a wider and a deeper study of English will reveal that what is suddenly denounced in Great Britain as the very latest Americanism, whether this be a variation in speech or in spelling, is shown to be really a survival of a previous usage of our language, and authorized by a host of precedents.

Of course it is idle to kick against the pricks of progress, and no doubt in due season Great Britain and her colonial dependencies will be content again to spell words that end in *er* as Shakspere and Ben Jonson and

Spenser spelled them. But when we get so far toward the orthographic millennium that we all spell *sepulcher*, the ghost of Thomas Campbell will groan within the grave at the havoc then wrought in the final line of 'Hohenlinden,' which will cease to end with even the outward semblance of a rime to the eye. We all know that

> On Linden, when the sun was low,
> All bloodless lay the untrodden snow,
> And dark as winter was the flow
>   Of Iser, rolling rapidly;

and those of us who have persevered may remember that with one exception every fourth line of Campbell's poem ends with a *y*,—the words are *rapidly, scenery, revelry, artillery, canopy*, and *chivalry*,—not rimes of surpassing distinction, any of them, but perhaps passable to a reader who will humor the final syllable. The one exception is the final line of the poem—

> Shall be a soldier's *sepulchre*.

To no man's ear did *sepulchre* ever rime justly with *chivalry* and *canopy* and *artillery*, altho Campbell may have so contorted his vision that he evoked the dim spook of a rime in his mind's eye. A rime to the eye is a sorry thing at best, and it is sorriest when it depends on an inaccurate and evanescent orthography.

Dr. Johnson was as illogical in his keeping in and leaving out of the *u* in words like *honor* and *governor* as he was in many other things; and the makers of later dictionaries have departed widely from his practice, those in Great Britain still halting half-way, while those in the United States have gone on to the bitter end. The illogic of the burly lexicographer is shown in his omission of the *u* from *exterior* and *posterior*, and his retention of it in the kindred words *interiour* and *anteriour*; this, indeed, seems like wilful perversity, and justifies Hood's merry jest about "Dr. Johnson's Contradictionary." The half-way measures of later British lexicographers are shown in their omission of the *u* from words which Dr. Johnson spelled *emperour, governour, oratour, horrour,* and *dolour,* while still retaining it in *favour* and *honour* and a few others.

The reason for his disgust generally given by the London man of letters who is annoyed by the "American spelling" of *honor* and *favor* is that these words are not derived directly from the Latin, but indirectly through the French; this is the plea put forward by the late Archbishop Trench. Even if this plea were pertinent, the application of this theory is not consistent in current British orthography, which prescribes the omission of the *u* from *error* and *emperor*, and its retention in *colour* and *honour*—altho all four words are alike derived from the Latin through the French. And this plea fails absolutely to account for the *u* which the British insist on preserving in *harbour* and in *neighbour*, words not derived from the Latin at all, whether directly or indirectly through the French. An American may well ask, "If the *u* in *honour* teaches etymology, what does the *u* in *harbour* teach?" There is no doubt that the *u* in *harbour* teaches a false etymology; and there is no doubt also that the *u* in *honour* has been made to teach a false etymology, for Trench's derivation of this final *our* from the French *eur* is absurd, as the old French was *our*, and sometimes *ur*, sometimes even *or*. Pseudo-philology of this sort is no new thing; Professor Max Müller noted that the Roman prigs used to spell *cena* (to show their knowledge of Greek), *coena*, as if the word were somehow connected with κοινή.

Thus we see that the *u* in *honour* suggests a false etymology; so does the *ue* in *tongue*, and the *g* in *sovereign*, and the *c* in *scent*, and the *s* in *island*, and the *mp* in *comptroller*, and the *h* in *rhyme*; and there are many more of our ordinary orthographies which are quite as misleading from a philological point of view. As the late Professor Hadley mildly put it, "our common spelling is often an untrustworthy guide to etymology." But why should we expect or desire spelling to be a guide to etymology? If it is to be a guide at all, we may fairly insist on its being trustworthy; and so we cannot help thinking scorn of those who insist on retaining a superfluous *u* in *harbour*.

But why should orthography be made subservient to etymology? What have the two things in common? They exist for wholly different ends, to be attained by wholly different means. To bend either from its own work to the aid of the other is to impair the utility of both. This truth is recognized by all etymologists, and by all students of language, altho it has not yet found acceptance among men of letters, who are rarely students of language in the scientific sense. "It may be observed," Mr. Sweet declares, "that it is mainly among the class of half-taught dabblers in philology that etymological spelling has found its supporters"; and he goes on to say that "all true philologists and philological bodies have uniformly denounced it as a monstrous absurdity both from a practical and a scientific point of view." I should never dare to apply to the late Archbishop Trench and the London journalists who echo his errors so harsh a phrase as Mr. Sweet's "half-taught dabblers in philology"; but when a fellow-Briton uses it perhaps I may venture to quote it without reproach.

As I have said before, the alleged "American spelling" differs but very slightly from that which prevails in England. A wandering New-Yorker who rambles through London is able to collect now and again evidences of orthographic survivals which give him a sudden sense of being in an older country than his own. I have seen a man whose home was near Gramercy Park stop short in the middle of a little street in Mayfair, and point with ecstatic delight to the strip of paper across the glass door of a bar proclaiming that *CYDER* was sold within. I have seen the same man thrill with pure joy before the shop of a *chymist* in the window of which *corn-plaisters* were offered for sale. He wondered why a British house should have *storeys* when an American house has *stories*; and he disliked intensely the wanton *e* wherewith British printers have recently disfigured *form*, which in the latest London typographical vocabularies appears as *forme*. This *e* in *form* is a gratuitous addition, and therefore contrary to the trend of orthographic progress, which aims at the suppression of all arbitrary and needless letters.

The so-called "American spelling" differs from the spelling which obtains in England only in so far as it has yielded a little more readily to the forces which make for progress, for uniformity, for logic, for common sense. But just how fortuitous and chaotic the condition of English spelling is nowadays both in Great Britain and in the United States no man knows who has not taken the trouble to investigate for himself. In England, the reactionary orthography of Samuel Johnson is no longer accepted by all. In America, the revolutionary orthography of Noah Webster has been receded from even by his own inheritors. There is no standard, no authority, not even that of a powerful, resolute, and domineering personality.

Perhaps the attitude of philologists toward the present spelling of the English language, and their opinion of those who are up in arms in defense of it, have never been more tersely stated than in Professor Lounsbury's most admirable 'Studies in Chaucer,' a work which I should term eminently scholarly, if that phrase did not perhaps give a false impression of a book wherein the results of learning are set forth with the most adroit literary art, and with an uninsistent but omnipresent humor, which is a constant delight to the reader:

"There is certainly nothing more contemptible than our present spelling, unless it be the reasons usually given for clinging to it. The divorce which has unfortunately almost always existed between English letters and English scholarship makes nowhere a more pointed exhibition of itself than in the comments which men of real literary ability make upon proposals to change or modify the cast-iron framework in which our words are now clothed. On one side there is an absolute agreement of view on the part of those who are authorized by their knowledge of the subject to pronounce an opinion. These are well aware that the present orthography hides the history of the word instead of revealing it; that it is a stumbling-block in the way of derivation or of pronunciation instead of a guide to it; that it is not in any sense a growth or development, but a mechanical malformation, which owes its existence to the ignorance of early printers and the necessity of consulting the convenience of printing-offices. This consensus of scholars makes the slightest possible impression upon men of letters throughout the whole great Anglo-Saxon community. There is hardly one of them who is not calmly confident of the superiority of his opinion to that of the most famous special students who have spent years in examining the subject. There is hardly one of them who does not fancy he is manifesting a noble conservatism by holding fast to some spelling peculiarly absurd, and thereby maintaining a bulwark against the ruin of the tongue. There is hardly one of them who has any hesitation in discussing the question in its entirety, while every word he utters shows that he does not understand even its elementary principles. There would be something thoroughly comic in turning into a fierce international dispute the question of spelling *honor* without the *u*, were it not for the depression which every student of the language cannot well help feeling in contemplating the hopeless abysmal ignorance of the history of the tongue which any educated man must first possess in order to become excited over the subject at all." ('Studies in Chaucer,' vol. iii., pp. 265-267.)

Pronunciation is slowly but steadily changing. Sometimes it is going further and further away from the orthography; for example, *either* and *neither* are getting more and more to have in their first syllable the long *i* sound instead of the long *e* sound which they had once. Sometimes it is being modified to agree with the orthography; for example, the older pronunciations of *again* to rime with *men,* and of *been* to rime with *pin,* in which I was carefully trained as a boy, seem to me to be giving way before a pronunciation in exact accord with the spelling, *again* to rime with *pain,* and *been* to rime with *seen.* These two illustrations are from the necessarily circumscribed experience of a single observer, and the observation of others may not bear me out in my opinion; but tho the illustrations fall to the ground, the main assertion, that pronunciation is changing, is indisputable.

No doubt the change is less rapid than it was before the invention of printing; far less rapid than it was before the days of the public school and of the morning newspaper. There are variations of pronunciation in different parts of the United States and of Great Britain, as there are variations of vocabulary; but in the future there will be a constantly increasing tendency for these variations to disappear. There are irresistible forces making for uniformity—forces which are crushing out Platt-Deutsch in Germany, Provençal in France, Romansch in Switzerland. There is a desire to see a standard set up to which all may strive to conform. In France a standard of pronunciation is found at the Comédie Française; and in Germany, what is almost a standard of vocabulary has been set in what is now known as *Bühnen-Deutsch.*

In France the Academy was constituted chiefly to be a guardian of the language; and the Academy, properly conservative as it needs must be, is engaged in a slow reform of French orthography, yielding to the popular demand decorously and judiciously. By official action, also, the orthography of German has been simplified and made more logical and brought into closer relation with modern pronunciation. Even more thorough reforms have been carried through in Italy, in Spain, and in Holland. Yet neither French nor German, not Italian, Spanish, or Dutch, stood half as much in need of the broom of reform as English, for in no one of these languages were there so many dark corners which needed cleaning out; in no one of them the difference between orthography and pronunciation so wide; and in no one of them was the accepted spelling debased by numberless false etymologies.

Beyond all question, what is needed on both sides of the Atlantic, in the United States as well as in Great Britain, is a conviction that the existing orthography of English is not sacred, and that to tamper with it is not high treason. What is needed is the consciousness that neither Samuel Johnson nor Noah Webster compiled his dictionary under direct inspiration. What is needed is an awakening to the fact that our spelling, so far from being immaculate at its best, is, at its best, hardly less absurd than the haphazard, rule-of-thumb, funnily phonetic spelling of Artemus Ward and of Josh Billings. What is needed is anything which will break up the lethargy of satisfaction with the accepted orthography, and help to open the eyes of readers and writers to the stupidity of the present system and tend to make them discontented with it.

(1892)

XIII
THE SIMPLIFICATION OF ENGLISH SPELLING

In a communication to a London review Professor W. W. Skeat remarked that "it is notorious that all the leading philologists of Europe, during the last quarter of a century, have unanimously condemned the present chaotic spelling of the English language, and have received on the part of the public generally, and of the most blatant and ignorant among the self-constituted critics, nothing but abusive ridicule, which is meant to be scathing, but is harmless from its silliness"; and it cannot be denied that the orthographic simplifications which the leading philologists of Great Britain and the United States are advocating have not yet been widely adopted. In an aggressive article an American essayist has sought to explain this by the assertion that phonetic-reform "is hopelessly, unspeakably, sickeningly vulgar; and this is an eternal reason why men and women of taste, refinement, and discrimination will reject it with a shudder of disgust." Satisfactory as this explanation may seem to the essayist, I have a certain difficulty in accepting it myself, since I find on the list of the vice-presidents of the Orthographic Union the names of Mr. Howells, of Colonel Higginson, of Dr. Eggleston, of Professor Lounsbury, and of President White; and even if I was willing to admit that these gentlemen were all of them lacking in taste, refinement, and discrimination, I still could not agree with the aggressive essayist so long as my own name was on the same list.

What strikes me as a better explanation is that given by the president of the Orthographic Union, Mr. Benjamin E. Smith, who has suggested that phonetic-reformers have asked too much, and so have received too little; they have demanded an immediate and radical change, and as a result they have frightened away all but the most resolute radicals; they have failed to reckon with the immense conservatism which gives stability to all the institutions of the English-speaking race. As Mr. Smith puts it, "there is a deep-rooted feeling that the existing printed form is not only *a* symbol but the *most fitting* symbol for our mother-tongue, and that a radical change must impair *for us* the beauty and spiritual effectiveness of that which it symbolizes."

A part of the unreadiness of the public to listen to the advocates of phonetic-reform has been due also to the general consciousness that pronunciation is not fixed but very variable indeed, being absolutely alike in no two places where English is spoken, and perhaps in no two persons who speak English. The humorous poet has shown to us how the little word *vase* once served as a shibboleth to reveal the homes of each of the four young ladies who came severally from New York and Boston and Philadelphia and Kalamazoo. The difference between the pronunciation of New York and Boston is not so marked as that between London and Edinburgh—or as that between New York and London. And the pronunciation of to-day is not that of to-morrow; it is constantly being modified, sometimes by imperceptible degrees and sometimes by a sudden change like the arbitrary substitution of *aither* and *naither* for *eether* and *neether*. Now, if pronunciation is not uniform in any two persons, in any two places, at any two periods, the wayfaring man is not to blame if he is in doubt, first, as to the possibility of a uniform phonetic spelling, and, second, as to its permanence even if it was once to be attained.

A glance down the history of English orthography discloses the fact that, however chaotic our spelling may seem to be now or may seem to have been in Shakspere's day, it is and it always has been striving ineffectively to be phonetic. Always the attempt has been to use the letters of the word to represent its sounds. From the beginning there has been an unceasing struggle to keep the orthography as phonetic as might be. This continuous striving toward exactness of sound-reproduction has never been radical or violent; it has always been halting and half-hearted: but it has been constant, and it has accomplished marvels in the course of the centuries. The most that we can hope to do is to help along this good work, to hasten this inevitable but belated progress, to make the transitions as easy as possible, and to smooth the way so that the needful improvements may follow one another as swiftly as shall be possible. We must remember that a half-loaf is better than no bread; and we must remind ourselves frequently that the greatest statesmen have been opportunists, knowing what they wanted, but taking what they could get.

We have now to face the fact that in no language is a sudden and far-reaching reform in spelling ever likely to be attained; and in none is it less likely than in English. The history of the peoples who use our tongue on both sides of the Atlantic proves that they belong to a stock which is wont to make haste slowly, to take one step at a time, and never to allow itself to be overmastered by mere logic. By a series of gradations almost invisible the loose confederacy of 1776 developed into the firm union of 1861, which was glad to grant to Abraham Lincoln a power broader than that wielded by any dictator. Even the abolition of the corn-laws and the adoption of free-trade in Great Britain, sudden as it may seem, was only the final result of a long series of events.

The securing of an absolutely phonetic spelling being impracticable,—even if it was altogether desirable,—the efforts of those who are dissatisfied with the prevailing orthography of our language had best be directed toward the perfectly practical end of getting our improvement on the instalment plan. We must seek now to have only the most flagrant absurdities corrected. We must be satisfied to advance little by little. We must begin by showing that there is nothing sacrosanct about the present spelling either in Great Britain or in the United States. We must make it clear to all who are willing to listen—and it is our duty to be persuasive always and never dogmatic—that the effort of the English language to rid itself of orthographic anomalies is almost as old as the language itself. We must show those who insist on leaving the present spelling undisturbed that in taking this attitude they are setting themselves in opposition to the past, which they pretend to respect. The average man is open to conviction if you do not try to browbeat him into adopting your beliefs; and he can be induced to accept improvements, one at a time, if he has it made plain to him that each of these is but one in a series unrolling itself since Chaucer. We must convince the average man that we want merely to continue the good work of our forefathers, and that the real innovators are those who maintain the absolute inviolability of our present spelling.

Even the vehement essayist from whom I have quoted already, and who is the boldest of later opponents of phonetic-reform, is vehement chiefly against the various schemes of wholesale revision. He himself refuses to make any modification,—except to revert now and again to a medievalism like *pædagogue*,—but he knows the history of language too well not to be forced to admit that a simplification of some sort is certain to be achieved in the future. "The written forms of English words will change in time, as the language itself will change," he confesses; "it will change in its vocabulary, in its idioms, in its pronunciation, and perhaps to some extent in its structural form. For change is the one essential and inevitable phenomenon of a living language, as it is of any living organism; and with these changes, slow and silent and unconscious, will come a change in the orthography." As we read this admirable statement we cannot but wonder why a writer who understands so well the conditions of linguistic growth should wish to bind his own language in the cast-iron bonds of an outworn orthography. We may wonder also why he is not consistent in his own practice, and why he does not spell *phænomenon* as Macaulay did only threescore and ten years ago.

Underneath the American essayist's objection to any orthographic simplification in English, and underneath the plaintive protests of certain British men of letters against "American spelling," so called, lies the assumption that there is at the present moment a "regular" spelling, which has existed time out of mind and which the tasteless reformers wish to destroy. For this assumption there is no warrant whatever. The orthography of our language has never been stable; it has always been fluctuating; and no authority has ever been given to anybody to lay down laws for its regulation. For a convention to have validity it must have won general acceptance at some period; and the history of English shows that there has never been any such common agreement, expressed or implied, in regard to English spelling. Some of the unphonetic forms which are most vigorously defended, as hallowed by custom and by sentiment, are comparatively recent; and others which seem as sacred have had foisted into them needless letters conveying false impressions about their origins.

That there is no theory or practice of English orthography universally accepted to-day is obvious to all who may take the trouble to observe for themselves. The spelling adopted by the 'Century Magazine' is different from that to be found in 'Harper's Magazine'; and this differs again from that insisted upon in the pages of the 'Bookman.' The 'Century' has gone a little in advance of American spelling generally, as seen in 'Harper's,' and the 'Bookman' is intentionally reactionary. In the United States orthography is in a healthier state of instability than it is in Great Britain, where there is a closer approximation to a deadening uniformity; but even in London and Edinburgh those who are on the watch can discover many a divergence from the strict letter of the doctrine of orthographic rigidity.

And just as there is no system of English spelling tacitly agreed on by all men of education using the English language at present, so there was also no system of English spelling consistently and continually used by our ancestors in the past. The orthography of Matthew Arnold differs a little, altho not much, from the orthography of Macaulay; and that in turn a little from the orthography of Johnson. In like manner the spelling of Dryden is very different from the spelling of Spenser, and the spelling of Spenser is very different from the spelling of Chaucer. At no time in the long unrolling of English literature from Chaucer to Arnold has there been any agreement among those who used the language as to any precise way in which its words should be spelled or even as to any theory which should govern particular instances. The history of English orthography is a record still incomplete of incessant variation; and a study of it shows plainly how there have been changes in every generation, some of them logical and some of them arbitrary, some of them helpful simplifications, and some of them gross perversities.

Thus we see that those who defend any existing orthography, which they choose to regard as "regular" and outside of which they affect to behold only vulgar aberration, are setting themselves against the example left us by our forefathers. We see also that those of us who are striving to modify our spelling in moderation are doing exactly what has been done by every generation that preceded us. To repeat in other words what I have said already, there is not any system of English orthography which is supported by a universal convention to-day or which has any sanctity from its supposed antiquity.

The opponents of simplification have been greatly aided by the general acceptance of this assumption of theirs that the advocates of simplification wanted to remove ancient landmarks, to break with the past, to introduce endless innovations. The best part of their case will fall to the ground when it is generally understood that the orthography of our language has never been fixed for a decad at a time. And this understanding of the real facts of the situation is likely to be enlarged in the immediate future by the wide circulation of many recent reprints of the texts of the great authors of the past in the exact spelling of the original edition. So long as we were in the habit of seeing the works of Shakspere and Steele, of Scott, Thackeray, and Hawthorne, all in an orthography which, if not uniform exactly, did not vary widely, we were sorely tempted to say that the spelling which was good enough for them is good enough for us and for our children.

But when we have in our hands the works of those great writers as they were originally printed, and when we are forced to remark that they spell in no wise alike one to the other; and when we discover that such uniformity of orthography they may have seemed to have was due, not to any theory of the authors themselves, but merely to the practice of the modern printing-offices and proof-readers—when these things are brought home to us, any superstitious reverence bids fair to vanish which we may have had for the orthography we believed to be Shakspere's and Steele's and Scott's and Thackeray's and Hawthorne's.

And one indirect result of this scholarly desire to get as near as may be to the masterpiece as the author himself presented it to the world, is that men of letters and lovers of literature—two classes hitherto strangely ignorant of the history of the English language and of the constant changes always going on in its vocabulary, in its syntax, and in its orthography—will at least have the chance to acquire information at first hand. Their resistance to simplification ought to become less irreconcilable when the men of letters, now its chief opponents, have discovered for themselves that there is not now and never has been any stable system of orthography. When they really grasp the fact that there has been no permanency in the past and that there is no uniformity in the present, perhaps they will show themselves less unwilling to take the next step forward. Just now they are rather like the Tories, who, as Aubrey de Vere declared, wanted to uninvent printing and to undiscover America.

The most powerful single influence in fixing the present absurd spelling of our language was undoubtedly Johnson's Dictionary, published in the middle of the eighteenth century. We cannot but respect the solid learning of Dr. Johnson and his indomitable energy; but the making of an English dictionary was not the task for which his previous studies had preëminently fitted him. Probably he would have succeeded better with a Latin dictionary; and indeed there is something characteristically incongruous in the spectacle of the burly doctor's spending his toil in compiling a list of the words in a language the use of which he held to be disgraceful in a friend's epitaph. Johnson was, in fact, as unfit a person as could be found to record English orthography, a task calling for a science the existence of which he did not even suspect, and for a delicacy of perception he lacked absolutely. In all matters of taste he was an elephantine pachyderm; and there are only a few of his principles of criticism which are not now disestablished.

Any one whose reading is at all varied and who strays outside of books printed within the past quarter-century, can find abundant evidence of the former chaos of English orthography. In Moxon's 'Mechanic Exercises,' published in 1683, for example, we read that "how well other Forrain languages are Corrected by the Author, we may perceive by the English that is Printed in Forrain Countries"; and this shows us that the phonetic form *forrain* is older than the unphonetic *foreign*. In the 'Spectator' (No. 510) Steele wrote *landskip* where we should now write *landscape*; in Addison's criticism of 'Paradise Lost,' contributed to the same periodical, we find *critick*, *heroick*, and *epick*; and whether Steele or Addison held the pen, *ribbons* were then always *ribands*.

On the title-page of the first edition of 'Robinson Crusoe,' published in 1719, we are told that we can read within "an account of how he was at last strangely delivered by *Pyrates*." Fielding, in the 'Champion' in 1740, tells us that "dinner soon follow'd, being a gammon of bacon and some chickens, with a most excellent apple-*pye*." In the same essay Fielding wrote that "our friends *exprest* great pleasure at our drinking"; and in 'Tom Jones' he wrote *profest* for *professed* (as we should now spell it). Here we discover that the nineteenth century is sometimes more backward than the eighteenth, *profest* and *exprest* being the very spellings which many are now advocating. Fielding also wrote *Salique* where we should now write *Salic*, as Wotton had written *Dorique* for *Doric* in a letter to Milton; and here the advantage is with us. So it is also in our spelling of the italicized word in the playbill of the third night of Mr. Cooper's engagement at the Charleston theater, Friday, April 18, 1796: "*Smoking* in the Theatre Prohibited."

Attention has already been called to Macaulay's *phœnomenon* (and to Professor Peck's *pædagogue*). The abolition of the digraph has been a protracted enterprise not yet completed. In a translation of Schlegel's 'Lectures on Dramatic Literature,' published in London early in the nineteenth century, I have found *æra* for *era*; and in the eighteenth century *economics* was *œconomics*. *Esthetic* has not yet quite expelled *æsthetic*, altho *anesthetic* seems now fairly established.

The Greek *ph* is also a stumbling-block. We write *phantom* on the one hand and *fancy* on the other, and either *phantasy* or *fantasy*; yet all these words are derived from the same Greek root. Probably *phancy* would seem as absurd to most of us as *fantom*. Yet *fantasy* has only recently begun to get the better of *phantasy*. The Italians are bolder than we are, for they have not hesitated to write *filosofia* and *fotografia*. To most of us *fotografer*, as we read it on a sign in Union Square, seems truly outlandish; and yet if our great-grandfathers were willing to accept *fancy* there is no logical reason why our great-grandchildren may not accept *fotografy*. There is no longer any logical basis for opposition on the ground of scholarship. Indeed, the scholarly opposition to these orthographic simplifications is not unlike the opposition in Germany to the adoption of the Roman alphabet by those who cling to the old Gothic letter on the ground that it is more German, altho it is in reality only a medieval corruption of the Roman letter. With those who speak German, as with those who speak English, the chief obstacle to the accomplishment of proposed improvements in writing the language is to be found in the general ignorance of its history—or perhaps rather in that conceited half-knowledge which is always more dangerous than modest ignorance.

To diffuse accurate information about the history of English orthography is the most pressing and immediate duty now before those of us who wish to see our spelling simplified. We must keep reminding those we wish to convince that we want their aid in helping along the movement which has in the past changed *musique* to *music*, *riband* to *ribbon*, *phantasy* to *fantasy*, *æra* to *era*, *phænomenon* to *phenomenon*, and which in the present is changing *catalogue* to *catalog*, *æsthetic* to *esthetic*, *programme* to *program*, *technique* to *technic*.

There never has been any "regular" spelling accepted by everybody, or any system of orthography sustained by universal convention. To assume that there is anything of the sort is adroitly to beg the very question at issue. There are always in English many words the spelling of which is not finally fixed; and these doubtful orthographies Professor Peck, for example, would decide in one way and Professor Skeat would decide in another. The most of Professor Peck's decisions would result in conforming his spelling to that which obtains in the printing-office of the London *Times*, but in several cases he would exercise the right of private judgment, spelling *pædagogue*, for example, and *Vergil*. But if he chooses to exercise the right of private judgment, he is estopped from denying this right also to Professor Skeat; and the moment either of them sets up the personal equation as a guide, all pretense of an accepted system vanishes.

It is our duty also to draw attention to the fact that it is a wholesome thing that there is no accepted system and that the orthography of our language should be free to modify itself in the future as it has in the past. It is this absence of system which gives fluidity and flexibility and the faculty of adaptation to changing conditions. The Chief Justice of England, when he addressed the American Bar Association, recorded his protest against a cast-iron code in law as tending to hinder legal development; and our language, like our law, must beware lest it lose its power of conforming to the needs of our people as these may be unexpectedly developed. Just as the conservatism of the English-speaking stock makes it highly improbable that any sweeping change in our spelling will ever be made, so the enterprise of the English-speaking stock, its energy and its common sense, make it highly improbable that any system will long endure which cramps and confines and prevents progress and simplification.

Finally, we must all of us bend our energies to combating the notion that, as Mr. Smith has put it, "the existing printed form is not only *a* symbol but the *most fitting* symbol of our mother-tongue." There is an almost superstitious veneration felt by most of us for the spellings we learnt at school; they seem to us sanctified by antiquity; and perhaps even an inquiry into the history of the language is not always enough to disestablish this reverence for false gods. Yet knowledge helps to free us from servitude to idols; and when we are told that the so-called "accepted spelling" has "dignity," we may ask ourselves what dignity there can be in the spelling of *harbour* with an inserted *u* which is not pronounced, which has been thrust in comparatively recently, and which is etymologically misleading.

In his effective answer to Mr. Herbert Spencer's argument against the metric system, President T. C. Mendenhall remarked that "ignorant prejudice" is not so dangerous an obstacle to human progress, nor as common, as what may be called "intelligent prejudice," meaning thereby "an obstinate conservatism which makes people cling to what is or has been, merely because it is or has been, not being willing to take the trouble to do better, because already doing well, all the while knowing that doing better is not only the easier, but is more in harmony with existing conditions. Such conservatism is highly developed among English-speaking people on both sides of the Atlantic." It is just such conservatism as this that those of us will have to overcome who wish to see our English orthography continue its lifelong efforts toward simplification.

To understand how unfortunate for the cause of progress it is when its leaders miscalculate the popular inertia and when they are therefore moved to demand more than seems reasonable to the people as a whole, we have only to consider the result of the joint action, in 1883, of the Philological Society of England and of the American Philological Association, in consequence of which certain rules were prepared to simplify our spelling. Here was a union of indisputable authorities in favor of an amended orthography; but unfortunately the changes suggested were both many and various. They were too various to please any but the most resolute radicals; and they were too many to be remembered readily by the great majority of every-day folk taking no particular interest in the subject. They included *theater, honor, advertize, catalog*; and had they not included anything else, or had they included only a very few similar simplifications, these spellings might have won acceptance in the past score of years, even in Great Britain; the same authorities would now be in a position to make a few further suggestions equally easy to remember, with a fair hope that these would establish themselves in turn.

Owing to this attempt to do too much all at once, the joint action of the two great philological organizations came to naught. Such effect as it had was indirect at best. It may have been the exciting cause of the so-called "Printers' Rules," which were approved and recommended by many of the leading typographers of the United States a few years later. These printers' rules were few and obvious. They suggested *catalog, program, epaulet, esthetic*—all of which have become more familiar of late. They suggested further *opposit, hypocrit*, etc., and also *fotograf, fonetic*, etc.; and these simplifications have not yet been adopted widely enough to prevent the words thus emended from seeming a little strange to all those who had paid no special attention to the subject. And these uninterested outsiders are the very people who are to be converted. To them and to them only must all argument be addressed. We may rest assured that we have slight chance of bringing over to our side any of those who have actually enlisted against us. We must not count on desertions from the enemy; we must enroll the neutrals at every opportunity.

Probably the most important action yet taken in regard to our orthography was that of the National Educational Association in formally adopting for use in all its official publications twelve simplified spellings—*program, tho, altho, thoro, thorofare, thru, thruout, catalog, prolog, decalog, demagog, pedagog*. These simplified spellings were immediately adopted in the 'Educational Review' and in other periodicals edited by members of the association. They are very likely to appear with increasing frequency in the school-books which members may hereafter prepare; and any simplified spelling which once gets itself into a school-book is pretty sure to hold its own in the future. After an interval of ten or fifteen years the National Educational Association will be in a position to consider the situation again; and it may then decide that these twelve words have established themselves in their new form sufficiently widely and firmly to make it probable that the association could put forward another list of a dozen more simplified spellings with a reasonable certainty that those also will be accepted.

The United States government appointed a board to decide on a uniform orthography for geographical names; and the recommendations of this body were generally in the direction of increased simplicity—*Bering* Straits, for example. The spellings thus officially adopted by the national government were at once accepted by the chief publishers of school text-books. And these makers of school-books also follow the rules formulated by a committee of the American Association for the Advancement of Science appointed to bring about uniformity in the spelling and pronunciation of chemical terms. Among the rules formulated by the committee and adopted by the association were two which dropped a terminal *e* from certain chemical terms entering into more general use. Thus the men of science now write *oxid, iodid, chlorid*, etc., and *quinin, morphin, anilin*, etc., altho the general public has not relinquished the earlier orthography, *oxide* and *quinine*. Even the word *toxin*, which came into being since the adoption of these rules by the associated scientists, is sometimes to be seen in newspapers as *toxine*.

Thus we see that there is progress all along the line; it may seem very slow, like that of a glacier, but it is as certain as it is irresistible. There is no call for any of us to be disheartened by the prospect. We may, indeed, each of us do what little we can severally toward hastening the result. We can form the habit of using in our daily writing such simplified spellings as will not seem affected or freakish, keeping ourselves always in the forefront of the movement, but never going very far in advance of the main body. We must not make a fad of orthographic amelioration, nor must we devote to it a disproportionate share of our activity—since we know that there are other reforms as pressing as this and even more important. But we can hold ourselves ready always to lend a hand to help along the cause; and we can show our willingness always to stand up and be counted in its favor.

(1898-1901)

www.ingramcontent.com/pod-product-compliance
Lightning Source LLC
Chambersburg PA
CBHW081111080526
44587CB00021B/3546